Here's How

Market Your College Degree

DOROTHY ROGERS
CRAIG BETTINSON

NTC LEARNINGWORKS

NTC/Contemporary Publishing Group

Library of Congress Cataloging-in-Publication Data
is available from the United States Library of Congress.

To Howard and Natalie Bettinson
Leslie Rogers and Joan Leopold

Originally published as *How to Market Your College Degree*
Cover illustrations by Art Glazer

Published by NTC LearningWorks
A division of NTC/Contemporary Publishing Group, Inc.
4255 West Touhy Avenue, Lincolnwood (Chicago), Illinois 60646-1975 U.S.A.
Copyright © 1992 by NTC/Contemporary Publishing Group, Inc.
All rights reserved. No part of this book may be reproduced, stored in a retrieval
system, or transmitted in any form or by any means, electronic, mechanical,
photocopying, recording, or otherwise, without the prior permission of
NTC/Contemporary Publishing Group, Inc.
Printed in the United States of America
International Standard Book Number: 0-8442-2623-8

99 00 01 02 03 04 VP 19 18 17 16 15 14 13 12 11 10 9 8 7 6 5 4 3 2 1

Contents

About the Authors   v
Foreword   vii
Preface   ix

Section I: What Is Marketing?

1 Marketing and You   3
Marketing Definitions   4
Your Strategic Marketing Plan   7

Section II: The Planning Stage

2 Self-Assessment   19
Work Values   20
Life Values   23
Skills   26
Interests   32

3 Market Analysis   40
Exploring Your Options   41
Business and Occupation Information
   Resources   47

Section III: The Human Product

**4 Self-Product Development and
Positioning   51**
Self-Product Mix Components   51
Positioning Yourself for Success   58

5 The Human Product Life Cycle   60
Stages of the Cycle   60
Two Career Stories   61

Section IV: Self-Promotion

6   **Networking   67**
Networking vs. Informational
   Interviewing   70
Networking in Action   71

7   **Resume and Cover Letter   73**
Tips for Creating Resumes   73
The Effective Cover Letter   100

8   **Interviewing   103**
Preparing for the Interview   107
The Interview Itself   111
After the Interview   115
Important Interview Points   115

Section V: Distribution

9   **Finding the Right Distribution
Channels   119**
The Place Factor   119
Major Distribution Channels   122

Section VI: Return on Investment

10   **Pricing   133**
Salary Information Resources   135
Negotiating   136
Fringe Benefits   137

Section VII: Postcampaign Behavior

11   **After You've Landed That
Job   143**
What Employers Expect   144
Office Politics   147
What Employees Expect   147
Moving On   148

About the
Authors

Dorothy S. Rogers is Vice-President for Institutional Advancement at New Hampshire College, where she previously served as director of cooperative education and director of the career development center as well as a member of the management/marketing faculty. Prior to her association with the college, she was a retail buyer.

Professor Rogers acts as a consultant to industry and other educational institutions, combining her knowledge of career development, recruitment, and marketing methodologies. Her clients have included such diverse organizations as Children's Orchard, a nationally franchised retailer; The New England Financial Services Company; the Dunkin Donuts franchise; and the National Commission for Cooperative Education.

The author of three books and numerous articles, Professor Rogers lectures and writes on a variety of marketing, retailing, and career development subjects and is a reviewer of marketing and retailing textbooks for a number of major publishers.

She holds a B.S. from Simmons College and has completed graduate course work at New York University.

Craig Bettinson is the former Associate Director of the Career Development Center at New Hampshire College. His other professional interests include private career counseling and ownership of a successful specialty retailing business.

Mr. Bettinson has taught career development, human relations, and organizational behavior at a number of colleges. He has chaired the New Hampshire College and University Council Career Advisors Consortium, as well as several committees of the Eastern College Personnel Officers.

He holds a B.A. from the University of Massachusetts at Lowell and a Master of Education in Industrial and Career Development Counseling from Northeastern University in Boston.

Foreword

Part of the education of a marketing student is devoted to the development of methods and techniques in market analysis. These skills include: opportunity identification, market research, market segmentation, alternative appraisal, and so forth. Few students seem to realize, however, that these same methods and techniques apply when it comes time to look for employment.

Finding that first professional position can seem like an insurmountable task. Closed doors and strange faces can shake the self-confidence of even the best prepared employment candidate. But finding a job is not impossible. Good planning, solid effort and patience will pay off. Students entering the job market must put all of their personal and professional skills to use. Another key factor is the proper design and preparation of resumes, cover letters, follow-up letters, and thank-you letters. And, just as a sales representative prepares for a presentation of a product, students must prepare for interviews.

The techniques that lead to a successful employment search are not mystical, nor are they particularly difficult. Most marketing majors have studied them and in some cases have used them. The critical factor is that they be applied effectively by all job hunters.

Study, evaluate and apply the techniques and suggestions presented in this book. Your career endeavors can be met with success if *you* take the necessary steps to make that happen.

Ginny Shipe
Director, Collegiate Chapter Services
American Marketing Association

Preface

Although *Here's How: Market Your College Degree* is primarily written for recent or soon-to-be college graduates who are starting the climb up the career ladder, it has just as much meaning for career changers of any age. *Here's How: Market Your College Degree* is the only in-depth career planning guide based on strategic marketing principles as applied to the human product, before, during, and after the job search.

Each chapter of the book is interspersed with examples and minicases that help drive home the plan, strategy, or tactic under discussion. We have tried to make our style readable and "user friendly," with little jargon. We hope that from page one the reader will believe that self-marketing is one of life's most exciting tasks. We strive to reinforce this belief throughout the book by translating marketing knowledge into career planning know-how.

Special Features   Section 1, "What Is Marketing?" discusses the marketing concept and marketing principles as they apply to the human product. Stress is placed on similarities between self-marketing and product or service marketing. Marketing terms are defined and illustrated so that the reader can use them effectively in a self-marketing campaign. The reader will also learn how to develop a strategic self-marketing plan and how to deal with the uncontrollable environmental variables—economic, political, and social—that impact all marketing planning.

Section 2, "The Planning Stage," starts with a segment on self-assessment and skills recognition that incorporates hands-on exercises with how-to planning information. Market analysis, a method of isolating targeted "niches" in the workplace and then matching one's skills to the needs in these targeted markets, brings the two major planning components together. After reading Section 2, the reader is ready to start developing an individually tailored self-marketing mix.

Section 3, "The Human Product," shows how a whole human product is developed from the proper "mixing" of its component parts: personality, skills, interests, and image. Once the product is complete, the focus turns to packaging; like any product, presentation is a key to success. Also included here is the subject of product positioning. This includes a complete discussion of those tactics that will help achieve recognition over the competition. The "Product Life Cycle" segment emphasizes human product development changes at different stages of one's career. A minicase carries two fictitious professionals through their life cycles.

Section 4, "Self-Promotion," looks at the various promotional tools that bring attention and interest to the human product and help create a desire for the product on the part of employers. Interview behavior is also a major topic. The three promotional tools—networking, the resume and the cover letter, and the interview—not only receive the most complete coverage, but also are illustrated with a variety of useful examples that can become the foundation upon which the reader's self-promotion campaign can be built.

Section 5, "Distribution," teaches the reader how to select those distribution channels that will lead to success. Because all products are different they cannot all travel the same employment road. The "short" direct channels and the longer channels, which include want ads, employment agencies, and on-campus recruiting programs, are differentiated, and the advantages and disadvantages of each are presented.

Section 6, "Return on Investment," by discussing the realities of pricing as applied to the human product, enables the reader to complete his or her strategic marketing plan. The worth and value placed on a college degree by the holder of the degree and by employers is not always the same. Uncontrollable variables can affect principal strategies at almost every stage of the human product life cycle. Knowing this will help in determining one's real worth in the marketplace.

Section 7, "Postcampaign Behavior," encourages the reader to continue using a marketing approach to career development and satisfaction throughout life. Transferable skills and repackaging are areas that always need attention. Use of different tactics and continued research are also essential. This final section points out the fact that since change is constant, self-marketing strategies must constantly change as one moves up the career ladder to success.

Here's How: Market Your College Degree would never have been published without Michael Urban. We wish to thank him, along with the editorial, design, and production staff of NTC/Contemporary Publishing Group.

Special thanks to all of our industry human resource collaborators: David Cassin, Kevin Joyce, Peter Marshall, Maureen Molan, and Jill Shea. Thanks also to Gladdy White, whose proofing and computer skills helped create our "final product," as well as to Gretchen and Jordan, Ann Kenney, Sue Gilbert, Kit Hayes, Charles Kovacs, Joe Barbeau, the New Hampshire College Career Development Center staff, and members of the New Hampshire College and University Council-Job Referral Service and Eastern College Personnel Officers.

Manchester, NH
Dorothy S. Rogers
Craig T. Bettinson

WHAT IS MARKETING?

Section I

Marketing and You 1

Although marketing as an academic discipline and the driving force behind modern business is a twentieth-century phenomenon, the practice has been around since the Garden of Eden, when Eve (the *original* marketer) saw the apple (the product) and convinced (promotion of the product) Adam (her target market) to take a bite. The distribution channel was the tree itself and the price—well, we all know what that was! The one step in the marketing process that Eve obviously missed was the planning stage. Without planning, even the most convincing marketing strategy, as in Eve's case, can fail, and instead of satisfaction and profit, the marketer can end up with hardship and loss.

Marketing must be looked at as a total process, a way of thinking that provides direction and focus and guides a company (or person) to satisfaction and profit because this dual goal was considered when the marketing blueprint was still on the drawing board. Although a strategic marketing plan cannot always guarantee success, the lack of one can almost always guarantee failure. In drawing up this plan for success, all marketers must (1) set goals, (2) determine strengths and weaknesses, (3) identify the uncontrollable factors in the environment that may affect attainment of their goals, and (4) set a strategic direction by matching strengths and weaknesses to the external environment.

It is necessary to understand the language of marketing before actually beginning a strategic marketing plan. All marketing plans have to have the proper frame of reference, regardless of the item or service under consideration. When the goal is to market oneself, this frame of reference is even more important than it is when marketing a product or service, since most people find it difficult to think of themselves in a marketing context, much less as the object of a strategic marketing plan.

Marketing Definitions

While reading the following definitions, begin to think of yourself as a human product, and you will then see why it is necessary to understand these terms. They will help you in establishing a plan to market yourself for both your first career job and for the rest of your professional life.

Marketing is the set of total functions that includes the planning, pricing, promotion, and distribution of an employer-demanded product for the dual purpose of satisfaction and profit for oneself and one's employer.

Here is an example. Michael *(product)* is a senior at a prestigious eastern university where he is majoring in business administration. Because he is concerned with the increasingly dynamic nature of the business environment, in developing his personal strategic marketing plan *(planning),* he decides to place major emphasis on his skills. He believes that his skills are flexible and could be sold in a variety of settings, not just to one type of employer. His next decision concerns *pricing.* After considering the expenses that must be covered by his salary (rent, food, utilities, a car, college loans, clothes, and recreation), he realizes that he needs to earn at least $22,000 in his first job in order to have a reasonable life-style. To achieve this financial goal, he decides to put together a resume that emphasizes his flexible skills. He also decides to purchase a navy blue suit with appropriate shirt, tie, shoes, and socks so that he will appear properly "packaged" for interviews with potential employers. Good resumes and interviews are, by far, the best form of *promotion* for the human product. Since Michael is constantly studying the economy and is tuned into the changing business environment, he decides to send his resume to and only accept interviews from employers located in the Midwest or Southwest, thereby limiting his *distribution* (sometimes referred to as *place*) to two major geographic areas in the United States.

After receiving offers from four firms, two in New Mexico, one in Indiana, and one in Illinois, Michael accepts the offer from a Fortune 200 firm in Illinois at a salary of $23,500. At his first year-end evaluation, he is told he has contributed a great deal to the success of the company's new product line and will receive a bonus as well as an increase in pay. Thus, the dual purpose of satisfaction and profit are realized, both for Michael and his employer.

Market is the group of employers who have the desire and the ability to hire and pay for the services of "human products." For example, all the potential employers who might have an interest in and openings for someone with Michael's education, experience, and skills make up his market.

Target market has two definitions. First, it refers to a relatively homogeneous group of employers to whom a potential employee wishes to appeal. Second, it consists of a relatively homogeneous group of customers or clients to whom an individual wishes to market his or her skills, as in an entrepreneurial enterprise. Continuing the example of Michael, all the potential employers who had an interest in and opportunity for someone with Michael's skills in the Midwest and Southwest fit into the first definition of a target market. For the second definition, we need to look at Michael after ten years with the employer who hired him when he graduated from the university. At that time, he decides to open up his own company. All the customers (old and new) who will buy from Michael's new company will make up his new target market.

Marketing mix is a person's unique blending of the four "P's" (*product, price, promotion,* and *place*) with the intent of being able to reach and satisfy his or her target market. When Michael (*product*), a unique individual in terms of his special combination of image, skills, education, and experience, decided, during the planning stage, that he needed a salary of $22,000 (*price*), that he would emphasize skills on his resume and in his interviews (*promotion*), and that he wanted to work only in the Midwest or Southwest (*place*), he was blending the four "P's" of marketing into a special mix that was uniquely his and that he hoped would reach and satisfy his target market. Because all individuals are unique, each person has the opportunity to create a marketing mix that differentiates himself or herself from everyone else seeking the same position.

Marketing concept is the philosophy that guides individuals in putting together their marketing mix so as to satisfy their potential employers, customers, or clients, and as a result, achieve profit (a good living and a good life). The marketing concept stresses satisfaction above profit and should be the basis for all self-marketing strategy development. In making the decisions that led him to create a "mix" that allowed him to reach his target and obtain an excellent job, Michael should have been guided by the marketing concept. From the previous examples, it would seem that Michael did pay heed to this concept. His first job paid more than enough to satisfy his basic needs, he was able to live in the geographic location of his choice, and after ten years was able to open his own business. From all indications, he has been able to make a good living and has a good professional life.

Market potential is the total number of possible opportunities for selling oneself within one's target markets. Michael's potential markets consisted of all the companies he isolated through research he performed while planning his "marketing mix," and who had opportunities for someone with his blend of skills, education, and experience.

Market share is the percentage of employment offers received by an individual as a result of his or her successful "marketing mix." Michael received offers from four companies during his job search. These four firms were his *share* of the total number of *potential* opportunities in his *target* markets.

Marketing channel is the route that individuals take from the beginning of the job search process until they are hired by an employer or open up their own business. During the distribution phase of his self-marketing process, Michael sent his resume to two hundred potential employers within his target markets. He interviewed with twelve companies, received offers from four, and finally accepted one. The route taken by his resumes as well as his various interviews represented stops in his personal marketing channel.

Your Strategic Marketing Plan

As you develop your personal strategic marketing plan, you must first decide upon your overall self-marketing strategy and then select the particular tactics that will help you achieve your strategic goal. Strategy should not be confused with tactics. A strategy is based on a clearly defined mission. Tactics support the strategy. Deciding which markets will become targets for a new shampoo is a strategic issue; deciding how to distribute and promote the shampoo to these markets is a tactical one.

Strategy indicates where you are heading; in other words, your career goals. Tactics answer questions of how to reach these goals. Set your goal as you begin your plan and never lose sight of this goal as you progress with your plan. It is the light at the end of the tunnel. It will keep you going if certain tactics fail or if you have to change tactics in midstream because of the sudden appearance of an uncontrollable variable, such as your reserve unit being called to active duty in a national emergency.

This brings up the subject of uncontrollable variables. No matter how well you think you understand the uncontrollables in the environment, no matter how many possible roadblocks you think you have considered when drawing up your strategic blueprint, certain elements in the environment that can affect your plan are uncontrollable because they are unexpected. It is impossible to factor in every unexpected change in the economy, in politics, or in the competition into the original plan.

Not being able to factor in every single uncontrollable variable in the environment when developing your self-marketing plan, however, does not mean that you are not in control. Even when the unexpected occurs, you should be able to reach your goal if you have been honest in assessing your strengths and weaknesses and in matching them to the needs in your target market or markets.

Controllable factors

A good marketer is pretty much in control of his or her own marketing mix—product, price, promotion, and place. If your strategic self-marketing plan is based on the principles of a good marketing mix, you should have a great deal of control over your own destiny.

Product. You, of course, are the product of your strategic marketing plan and since marketing textbooks teach that the marketer has control over the development of his or her product, it can be reasoned that you have complete control over your own career development. If, therefore, you thoroughly research your target markets, you should be able to make yourself into the perfect product for these markets. Right? Not always! First of all, no one is perfect. Second, those old uncontrollables are lurking in the background, and as the economy or the competition changes, it is possible that your "perfect" skills may have to stand the test of transferability.

The best way to guarantee yourself as a marketable product is to analyze your strengths and weaknesses. This is no easy task. Self-assessment alone, no matter how honest, does not always help you to present yourself as others see you, though it does provide a solid foundation for your development process. A good tactic is to bring others into this stage of your strategic plan. Charles Handy, who recently was a visiting professor at the London Business School and is a writer on organizational change, has suggested that in order to free up your thinking about yourself, you should go to twenty people you know and ask each one to tell you one thing you do well. Often, the results are interesting and unexpected. What if you were the star of your advertising class or your agency (if a job changer), and in asking twenty people what you do well, not one mentioned your advertising expertise but instead said you were creative, good at organizing people and ideas, and had good leadership skills. These answers would properly expand your horizons and allow you to think beyond the advertising field as your one and only career option. While self-analysis is the basis for self-product development, input from others helps create an even better product.

During the product development stage, it is also necessary to consider "packaging." Even though this is discussed in-depth later on, it is important to mention here that the way you "package" yourself can say a great deal to prospective "buyers." Your image, just like the image of a new product on display in a department store filled with competing products, can either indicate your strengths or your weaknesses, can differentiate you from the rest of the pack, or can say "Mary is just another face in the crowd." How you dress, speak, walk, sit, shake hands; how you sound on the telephone; the appearance of your resume—all these things represent you—the person—and they all can say, pick me or put me back on the shelf.

Pay particular attention to this phase of your self-product development. Rejection based on image is not easy to overcome, and just like the new product that no one was drawn to, you could end up on the marked-down rack.

Differentiate yourself. Indicate the difference between you and the rest of the human products. When interviewing, display those two rare elements always mentioned by employers: enthusiasm and energy. You would be surprised at the number of job candidates who lack these qualities. Don't be one of them.

Another way to differentiate yourself is by your clothing. When analyzing your target markets, be sure you study the correct professional look in each one. Select your interviewing wardrobe with this "look" in mind, but then put yourself together so that even though you fit the market's image, you do not look like a clone. Your "frame" (suit or dress) should be selected because it is one that is acceptable in your target markets, but the "portrait" inside the frame (color, fit, accessories) will make you memorable if it is differentiated from the rest.

Price. Only you can determine the salary range that is acceptable for you. Having a sense of your own value is perfectly appropriate in the real world. So even if you're not driven by the dollar, a concern about salary is healthy and natural. You cannot, however, decide what any job or person is worth to an employer. Only an employer can make that decision.

Many people confuse their own sense of worth with their market value. The salary you decide you need when developing your mix is based on a self-analysis that considers your particular education, experience, skills, image, personality, financial obligations, and desire for a certain life-style. Although these factors become vital components of the price you set on yourself as a human product, they are not the same factors that influence the potential buyers (employers).

Employers want their employees to be happy and do give some consideration to an individual's needs when determining salary levels, but they are primarily driven by their total salary costs as well as by supply versus demand (the ratio of availability of good human products to job openings). It is the employer who sets market value.

When you place a price on yourself, be sure it is in keeping with your market value in your target market or markets. This can only be determined after thorough market research. The price portion of your marketing mix has to be realistic in order for your plan to succeed; only a realistic view will help you control the price variable.

Promotion. The best product in the world will not sell unless people know about it. Self-promotion, therefore, is as vital to the human product as advertising, visual displays, and promotional events are to consumer goods, and personal selling is to industrial items. "Wishing" will not make it so! Employers rarely come looking for specific individuals, no matter how great each one believes he or she is.

The good news is that you, the product, are in control of your own self-promotion. You can receive advice from others, but in the final analysis, it is your resume, your networking efforts, and your skills at interviewing that will determine your success in the marketplace.

If you can get your potential customers to believe in you, it is an easy task to market your product or service. Even salespeople who promote well-known merchandise or services often fail if they have not convinced their customers of their own personal value, honesty, and product knowledge. Selling oneself is a preliminary tactic in selling all goods and services, but it is the major self-promotion task when the product to be sold is *you.*

A three-pronged tactical approach is used in self-promotion. Later on in *Here's How: Market Your College Degree*, these three "prongs"—resumes, networking, and interviewing—are discussed in detail.

Just like an attractive store window that customers believe shows samples of the merchandise inside, a good resume will allow prospective employers to get a glimpse of the human product who prepared the resume. If a resume, like a store window, falsely represents "merchandise" however, customers will not buy; they will also resent the misrepresentation. Their first "shopping visit" will probably be their last, whether the merchandise is clothing, appliances, or YOU.

A resume that is not attractive will not lead to an interview, but attractiveness is only one element of a marketable resume. It must also offer a concise and honest history of the "product" being described. Like the store window, an attractive resume may result in a first interview, but there will never be a second if any of the facts (which can easily be checked in our information society) have been even slightly altered and indicate misrepresentation from the individual who put the resume together.

A good honest resume, step one, should lead to step two, the interview. The interview is the time to put your best self-promotional foot forward. It is your chance to look and act confident and speak intelligently and knowledgeably. As with any salesperson presenting a product to a potential buyer, this face to face "sales pitch" is your opportunity to shine.

The third prong of your three-pronged tactical approach to self-promotion is networking. Networking is one of the best ways of letting the world know that you are looking for employment. Wishing may not make it so, but networking can.

Distribution. Even if you have done a great job of controlling the first three elements of your personal marketing mix, satisfaction and profit will still not be within your grasp without proper distribution. Which distribution channels can the human product travel, you ask? Ones that, at least in terms of their varying length, are not dissimilar from the channels taken by nonhuman products. You can take the short route by writing to or calling potential employers directly (manufacturer to consumer) or you can go through indirect channels such as job fairs or employment agencies (manufacturer to wholesaler and/or retailer to consumer). Many job seekers use every available channel, short or long, for the goal of self-distribution is market coverage.

Possible Distribution Channels for the Human Product

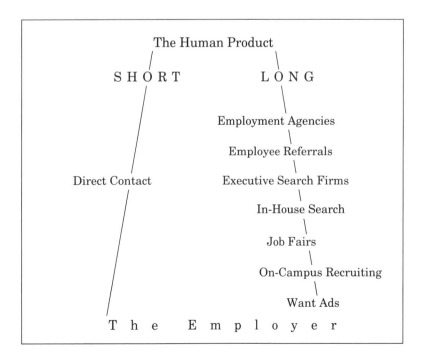

Be sure and study all available channels before deciding which ones to use and which ones to avoid. Only through research can you discover, for example, which employers only hire people who approach them directly, which employers hire from want ads in trade papers, which employers use professional employment agencies, and which employers hire through on-campus recruiting.

It is important to understand the various and different routes that your resume and you can travel on the road to employment, as your marketing mix is not complete until distribution plans are complete.

A final statement concerning the marketing mix—remember, product, price, promotion, and place are yours to control. In exercising this control, develop a realistic and honest mix, and your self-marketing plan should be able to withstand the many uncontrollable elements that you will inevitably meet along the job search road.

Uncontrollable factors

As previously stated, there are environmental elements over which individuals have little control, yet within whose framework they must develop their personal marketing mix. Inflation, recession, changing demographics, population shifts, new legislation, advancing technology, social movements, and existing legal constraints all affect the job market and must be considered when completing a strategic self-marketing plan. Learn to expect the unexpected. All during the development of your personal plan, keep a constant eye out for changes in the environment. Accept the fact that this is an ever-changing world, and that change is normal. When analyzing your strengths and weaknesses, think of the uncontrollable variables you may have to face. When studying the environment, keep an open mind and be ready to adjust your strategic plan at any moment.

Your personal marketing mix must reflect both an understanding and acceptance of change. You cannot sell a 1960s image in a twenty-first century world. You cannot price yourself high if your original target industry is facing massive lay-offs. You cannot promote yourself with a three-page resume in a society where recruiters spend only twenty seconds reading each of the two thousand resumes they have received for forty available jobs. And you would certainly be wasting your time distributing your resumes in geographic areas where there has been a sudden downturn in the economy.

Economic variables. There is no better indicator of the economy than the help-wanted section of your city's Sunday newspaper. Reading these ads will help you feel the employment pulse. In 1989, most help-wanted sections were thick with offers of varied opportunities in a variety of businesses. By 1991, a much thinner section offered fewer opportunities and less variety. There was also a total absence of ads from certain industries.

The everyday expression of economic theory can be found in employment trends, so when there is a recession and employment is down, your strategic plan, drawn up during a period of high employment, has to be adjusted. Starting salaries, like employment trends, also reflect economic theory, especially the theory of supply and demand. When the economy is growing and employment is high, you are more likely to get your "price" since demand is greater than supply. When supply is greater than demand, however, and there is a larger pool of applicants to choose from, it will be the employers and not the marketer who call the shots.

Sociological variables. Variables in society that bring about demographic and cultural life-style changes can also affect your personal marketing strategy. Therefore, when developing a marketing mix, consider the following. Each one can impact your plan:

- Population shifts: There are generally more job opportunities in heavily populated geographic areas than in sparsely populated areas. Of course, there are exceptions. If a specific high-tech company moves to northern Montana (low population) and you are interested in a job in the high-tech industry, northern Montana should be on your list.

- The changing age mix: As the baby boom generation ages and more people work beyond traditional retirement age, competition from older workers for all available jobs becomes a variable that demands attention.

- Higher education levels: More educated people mean that employers have a better pool of candidates from which to select employees. This means stiffer competition.

- More women in the workplace: Merit, not sex, is often the deciding factor in today's world. There was a time when certain jobs were "men's" jobs and others were "women's" jobs. Today, the person who best fits the job will most likely get it, regardless of sex.

- An emerging global economy: The need to speak more than one language is fast becoming a necessity for employment and most certainly for advancement in multinational companies. A study of different cultures is also essential when dealing in foreign markets. It is difficult to work with or sell to people whose customs you do not understand. How can you expect to sell products to the Japanese if you do not understand either their language or their business practices? How can an employment manager make hiring decisions for a new plant in Germany if he or she has neglected to study the problems of integrating people from the East into the West? A global perspective is the only perspective to take if you are seeking employment in any multinational firm.

Both employers and employees have a considerably different set of values than they did a decade ago. It is these values and attitudes that bring about changes in hiring practices and must be considered in a strategic self-marketing plan. For example, there is recognition and respect for differing origins as well as an absence of stigma concerning divorce or the single state. There is concern for the environment and for health and fitness, and because of the great emphasis, worldwide, on technology and information, value is placed on an information rather than on an industrial society.

The values, behavior patterns, and attitudes of a society become the guideposts that self-marketers must follow in order to meet the needs and preferences of the culture within which they seek employment. No one can market himself or herself in a vacuum.

Political influences. Political events often bring about enormous changes that affect the day-to-day operations of all businesses. A treaty between the United States and Russia can open new employment doors while war in the Middle East will close other ones. The emergence of women and minorities as political groups and a new administration in Washington can have ramifications in the workplace that go far beyond the immediate political events. After a women has run for vice-president of the United States and a black American has been a serious contender for the presidency, anyone can now occupy the executive suite.

U.S. trade with China, one European Economic Community, the reunification of East and West Germany, and the disintegration of the U.S.S.R. are all political events that have affected the world economy. Whatever affects the world economy affects the number and nature of jobs in that economy. Whatever affects the number and nature of global jobs affects the methods used to find and get those jobs. Whatever affects job-search methodologies requires research and study. A self-marketing plan that ignores the ramifications of political events, even local ones, cannot be adjusted to meet the needs of the marketplace. As part of your preparation process, be sure and study local, regional, national, and world politics.

Legal constraints. In every employment situation the law—local, state, or federal—is a determinant of strategy and imposes limits beyond which employers cannot venture. Study the legal framework within which employers must function so that you, a potential employee, can be sure that your marketing mix also fits the frame. Below is a sample list of legislation with which you should be familiar.

- 1938—Fair Labor Standards Act. Established minimum wages.

- 1963—Equal Pay Act. Required compliance with regulations on child labor and employee health and safety.

- 1964—Civil Rights Act, Title VII. Required equal pay for similar work, regardless of sex, race, color, religion, or national origin.

- 1968—Age Discrimination in Employment Act. Prevented discrimination against employing anyone on the basis of age; extended retirement age to seventy.

- 1986—Tax Reform Act. Plugged many former tax loopholes, consolidated fifteen tax brackets into two.

Technological changes. Since the industrial revolution, no other phenomenon has had such far-reaching effects on business and industry as the technological revolution. It is almost impossible for either a small business or a large one, a for-profit or a not-for-profit business, to operate without technological aids ranging from copy machines to fax machines to computers. Information in ever-greater amounts is in constant demand and growing.

Because the computer is indispensable for success in business, computer knowledge is an indispensable ingredient of your product mix. You may not be able to control the daily technological advances in an information world, but you can control the way you, the product, are preparing to function in this information society.

As you begin planning your self-marketing strategy, remember that your degree is only as important as the plan that brings it (and you) to the attention of potential employers. A degree from the most prestigious college or university in the world will not sell the person who possesses it unless it is used as the cornerstone of a well-thought-out strategic marketing plan.

Section II

THE PLANNING STAGE

Peter Marshall,
Partner, Cooper and Lybrand

I remember thinking during my junior year in college that the time was near when I would have to market myself in order to get a job. I had only recently learned what a Certified Public Accountant did and was obviously plunging ahead toward a career that I knew little about. However, that did not stop me, nor should it ever stop any of you.

Until this time in your life, many of your decisions have probably been more haphazard than formalized or planned; certainly mine were. That is why it is important to recognize that some planning will be required to get you from where you are today to that job of tomorrow.

One of my job functions over the past ten years has been on-campus recruiting. I am also involved in on-campus seminars on recruiting techniques. As a recruiter, I appreciate and value the need to plan the process of one's life with as much care as possible.

This section of *How to Market Your College Degree* is on planning. I cannot emphasize enough the positive impact that a well-planned interview/presentation has on a recruiter. In the interviewing process, there is little time or opportunity for you to differentiate yourself from the others—that is, *your competition*. Somehow, some way, you need to present yourself in the best light and in some cases, a different light. The only assured way to accomplish this is through thorough planning. I refer to the need to know who you are, what your strengths and weaknesses are, and why you made the life's decisions that you have made to date, such as summer job decisions, the college you selected, and the courses you took. This self-assessment is the critical first step in planning your career-selection strategy. As a next step, it is important to study the markets, what type of position you want, what culture/environment you wish to work in, what geographic region you want to live in, and why.

For many of you who are about to market your college degree, in-depth planning probably seems to be an overwhelming task. In hindsight, I had no idea of the impact of each action that I took. I don't believe, however, that the lack of experience or ability ever negates the need to pursue the planning process and to use whatever means are available to make the most educated decision that you can make. This process and its results are an integral part of who you are, and this, I believe, will be a critical component of your individual success.

One further point of advice. After having planned your career-entry process, periodically retest the key premises. If they still hold true, persevere. Don't give up. Tenacity is still a virtue.

Self-Assessment

You now know that creating a marketing mix involves completing a thorough self-assessment. You also know that if you are to become a marketable product this assessment must point out your strengths and weaknesses. Self-assessment, which includes looking at your work and life values, skills, and interests, will be discussed in detail throughout this section. In addition, there are exercises provided for self-discovery. Regardless of how confident you are in your career choice and immediate career plans, complete the exercises. The information gained will be helpful in constructing your resume and useful in the interview process, two of the major self-promotion tactical tools.

Some college graduates are in the enviable position of knowing exactly what they would like to do immediately after completing their college degrees. They proceed through the job-search process while still in school, often taking advantage of internship or co-operative education opportunities, and begin their careers soon after graduation. These people are among the minority, so don't worry if you are not one of them. Many graduates postpone their careers, others take any job they can get, and some continue their education in graduate school. Because you may experience pressure from your family to utilize your college education or pressure from banks looking for loan payments, you may feel forced to make a decision about your career. But only make a career decision if it is appropriate for you. You and you alone control your future. If graduate school or a temporary job seems the best option at the time, follow your own, not someone else's, needs.

Self-assessment is just as necessary for those who aren't sure of what they can or want to do with their degrees as it is for those who are. The process opens up new doors and creates new options. Having these options as you begin the job search is critical since very few people are able to land the job of their dreams first time out. Graduates of recent years have learned very quickly that their ideal job was not there waiting for them upon graduation. Those who went through self-assessment and identified different options were able to sell themselves well, and as a result, find satisfying, profitable employment.

Work Values   Your work values should embody all that is of importance to you in your career. It is essential to develop yourself into the type of "product" that will allow you to work in career fields and for organizations where your values can be met and you can realize personal happiness and job satisfaction. Note the following example.

Jill is a college graduate employed in a retail store. Jill has worked much of her college life as a retail intern. During her senior year she completed a work-values exercise and learned that her top values were pleasant co-workers, leadership, and prestige. In what better field than retailing could she meet these values?

Therefore when Jill graduated and was offered a full-time job as store manager with her current employer, she accepted. Soon after Jill began her new position, it became evident to her that her relationships with her peers had changed. They were not as friendly as they had been when she was "one of them." Jill learned that in her new position she had a conflict in values and because of this conflict was not going to be able to meet her need for friendly relationships on the job. As manager, she was required to "lay down the law" or run the risk of losing her position. She decided that it would be best to keep the job and to develop outside relationships to fulfill her social needs, which could not be met in her new work environment, since her other two values, leadership and prestige, were being fulfilled as store manager.

Work-values exercise   To complete the work-values exercise that follows read the list briefly in order to familiarize yourself with the range of these values. Go through the list a second time and rate each of the statements according to the following rating scale:

Rating Scale

1. An absolute must in your life

2. Important

3. Not important at all

Once you have completed the list, go back again and narrow down your top five value choices. You may have many number 1's. It's advisable to begin with them and if necessary proceed to the 2's. The first five are your current top work values!

How important is it to have?

_____ independence/autonomy	opportunity to work with little direction
_____ flexibility	opportunity to choose your own time schedule
_____ change/variety	opportunity for different tasks and settings
_____ risks	opportunity to challenge established order
_____ job security	opportunity to work in a stable organization
_____ physical challenge	opportunity to utilize physical capabilities
_____ mental challenge	opportunity to utilize intelligence and be creative
_____ precise work	opportunity for work that leaves little room for error
_____ decision-making functions	opportunity to choose what you do and how you do it
_____ teamwork	opportunity for working as part of a group
_____ truth/knowledge	opportunity to gain understanding and knowledge
_____ expertise/skill	opportunity to work with expert or leader in field
_____ creativity/innovation	opportunity to develop new ideas or programs
_____ social contributions	opportunity to improve society
_____ socioeconomic status	opportunity to gain money and other material objects
_____ achievement/recognition	opportunity to receive public recognition for work
_____ ethics/morality	opportunity to follow ethical standards
_____ self-expression	opportunity to express your self-concept
_____ life-style of choice	opportunity to lead life by your rules
_____ solitary work	opportunity for minimal contact with others
_____ interpersonal relations	opportunity for lots of people contact
_____ help for others	opportunity to serve the needs of others
_____ leadership/management functions	opportunity to plan, lead, organize, and control others
_____ advancement potential	opportunity to climb the ladder
_____ friendly co-workers	opportunity for having friends at work
_____ good productivity	opportunity for measured results

Record your top five work values here.

TOP WORK VALUES

1. _____

2. _____

3. _____

4. _____

5. _____

What does your list say about you? Have you noticed a theme that may be helpful in career decision making? Remember that values change over time, so that you may have to revisit the experience as you move through your career life cycle.

Life Values

Life values are those things that you prize and place value on today. For some, a career is a top value; for others, raising a family or self-discovery is a priority. It is essential that you be honest with yourself about the importance of your career. If a career is not something that you value then you may not be willing to make the investment in the process subscribed to in this book. After all, developing your personal marketing plan involves a lot of hard work and dedication.

Life-values exercise

Complete the life-values exercise to assess your current life values. Begin by reading through the life-values list to familiarize yourself with the range of these values. Go through the list a second time and rate each of the statements using the following rating scale:

Rating Scale

1. An absolute must in your life
2. Important
3. Not important at all

Once you have completed the list, go back again and narrow down your top ten choices. You may have many number 1's. Begin with them and proceed to the 2's if necessary. The first ten are your current top values in life! Share your results with friends; maybe they have some thoughts that could be helpful. Come back to your list at a later date and reevaluate.

How important is?

_____ owning a home	_____ experiencing culture
_____ wearing fashionable clothes	_____ growing emotionally
_____ having open relationships	_____ being an individual
_____ having harmonious relations	_____ having power and authority
_____ stretching yourself mentally	_____ having good food and beverage
_____ having material goods	_____ having a great deal of money
_____ being challenged	_____ having permanent employment
_____ being financially secure	_____ being creative
_____ having a close family	_____ having a good marriage
_____ having close friends	_____ learning and gaining knowledge
_____ being productive	_____ being spiritual
_____ feeling your life counts	_____ being an authority in your field
_____ using skills and abilities	_____ being famous
_____ continuing self-discovery	_____ being politically active
_____ being close to nature	_____ being free and independent
_____ feeling your work counts	_____ having integrity
_____ empowering others	_____ being playful
_____ using your mind	_____ living a long life
_____ working for important causes	_____ working with a group
_____ being safe	_____ having a career
_____ taking risks	_____ having adventure and excitement
_____ accepting physical challenges	_____ having and making order
_____ supporting justice for all	_____ having leisure
_____ helping others	_____ being a hard worker

TOP LIFE VALUES

1. _____

2. _____

3. _____

4. _____

5. _____

6. _____

7. _____

8. _____

9. _____

10. _____

What does your list say about you? Is there a theme that may be helpful in career decision making? Will a successful career assist you to meet your life values?

Skills The importance of skill development has gained wide recognition in recent years. Employers pay employees for the skills they contribute to their bottom line and to their customers' satisfaction. The more valuable the skills or abilities you have to offer an employer, the more likely you are to get hired and paid what you would like. You must be aware of the skills you possess and know how you can use them in your career decision-making process. This way you will begin to understand what you can offer to an employer. If you do not have the skills required for a particular job, then you must set out to develop them through work experiences, cooperative education, volunteer positions, continued education, participation in activities both on campus and in the general community, hobbies, or life in general. The skills exercise chart on page 27 provides you with an opportunity to identify your top skill areas.

There are three major skill categories:

1. Functional
2. Personal
3. Work content

By looking at each you will discover the differences.

Functional skills are those that may or may not be associated with a specific job. Examples of these are answering the telephone, maintaining schedules, collecting data, and diagnosing and responding to problems. These are called functional skills because they are tasks or functions of a job.

Personal skills are personal attributes. They might also be described as personality traits. The ability to learn quickly, the ability to pay close attention to detail, task orientation, self-direction, congeniality, and cooperativeness are some examples of adaptive skills.

Work-content skills are specific and specialized to one job. Bookkeeping is done by bookkeepers, assigning grades is done by teachers, interpreting EKG's is done by specific medical practitioners, and employee training is done by human resource specialists.

Skills-assessment exercise

Assessing skills has been popularized through the work of Richard Bolles in his book *What Color Is Your Parachute?* Others such as Howard Figler and Tom Jackson have reinforced the need for identifying skills as an important step in the job search.

To complete your skills assessment think about all of the positions you have held. Be sure to include volunteer and nonpaid positions. Reflect back to your high school and college years and identify all of your affiliations and memberships. What have you done in the community? What are your hobbies? Your answers will provide a clue as to the skills you possess. Go through the following inventory and write next to each skill what you have done to develop that skill. When you complete the list go back and ask yourself if this is a particular skill that you enjoy using and would like to incorporate into your career choice; if so, circle it.

Functional

assembling _____

constructing _____

having manual dexterity _____

repairing _____

reading _____

copying _____

writing/communicating _____

teaching/training _____

editing _____

observing/surveying _____

examining/inspecting _____

diagnosing/determining _____

taking inventory _____

calculating/computing _____

managing money _____

researching information _____

solving problems _____

prioritizing _____

diagnosing _____

systematizing _____

comparing _____

testing and screening _____

appraising and evaluating _____

counseling and guiding _____

advising _____

initiating new ideas, projects _____

organizing _____

leading and directing others _____

promoting change _____

making decisions _____

performing before a group _____

selling and promoting _____

negotiating and persuading _____

administering _____

using what others have developed _____

following through on plans or instructions _____

attending to details _____

classifying and recording information _____

filing and retrieving _____

coordinating _____

questioning _____

explaining _____

interpreting _____

translating _____

interviewing _____

investigating _____

listening _____

budgeting _____

compiling _____

updating _____

controlling _____

recording _____

developing models _____

predicting _____

troubleshooting _____

estimating _____

displaying _____

processing _____

distributing _____

delegating _____

recruiting _____

managing _____

mediating _____

monitoring _____

planning _____

reviewing _____

Personal

using precision/speed _____

using muscular coordination _____

being physically active _____

having memory for words _____

paying attention to detail _____

having number memory _____

manipulating numbers rapidly _____

having foresight _____

sizing up people or situations _____

having insight _____

acting on gut reactions _____

visualizing the third dimension _____

analyzing and dissecting _____

organizing and classifying _____

abstracting and conceptualizing _____

imagining _____

inventing and creating _____

designing and developing _____

improvising _____

adapting and improving _____

helping others _____

being sensitive to others' feelings _____

listening _____

developing rapport _____

caring and conveying warmth _____

understanding _____

drawing out people _____

offering support _____

demonstrating empathy _____

motivating _____

sharing credit _____

raising others' self-esteem _____

healing and curing _____

taking the first move in relationships _____

taking risks _____

dealing with pressure _____

Work Content

keeping financial records _____

composing music _____

playing instruments/singing _____

sculpturing _____

taking pictures and creating architectural blueprints __

painting, decorating _____

expressing feelings through the body _____

writing poetry and plays _____

sketching _____

auditing _____

making layouts _____

programming _____

rehabilitating _____

teaching _____

fund raising _____

group facilitating _____

Interests   Identifying your interests is important in the planning portion of your strategic self-marketing plan. This can be done in many different ways. Most people can easily identify careers in which they have little interest, but few are able to name more than one or two specific career choices that are of interest to them. To do this, research is necessary, even though it may be the last thing in which you want to get involved. One too many papers throughout your degree program has probably soured you on all research and completing a self-assessment for your career plan is something you would like to skip. Not possible! Without research into careers that interest you, you cannot develop a successful self-marketing mix, and without planning a mix that considers your strengths and weaknesses, as well as the uncontrollables in the environment, you might end up like Eve. The planning stage is not the place to skimp on research. Although individuals may have their own preferred way of identifying their own interests, the resources and exercises that follow are some of the options available for you when identifying your special career interests: *The Guide for Occupational Exploration, The Strong Campbell Vocational Interest Inventory, The Harrington O'Shea Career Decision Making System,* your childhood work fantasy, your picture of the perfect day, and your past work volunteering history.

Guide for Occupational Exploration

The Guide For Occupational Exploration, which is available in public libraries and through the Department of Labor, offers a very stimulating and enjoyable method for self-career exploration. It is a personal favorite because "The World of Work" is divided into 12 interest areas, 66 work groups, and 348 subgroups.

The guide organizes all occupations in the United States into twelve areas on the basis of worker interest. The twelve interest areas correspond to the interest factors identified from research in interest measurement conducted by the Division of Testing of the U.S. Employment Service. The interest factors listed represent the interests of employed individuals. Examples of interest areas include:

- Artistic: an interest in creative expression, feelings, or ideas.

- Selling: an interest in bringing others to a particular point of view by personal persuasion, using sales and promotion techniques.

- Humanitarian: an interest in helping others with their mental, spiritual, social, physical, or vocational needs.

The twelve interest areas are further divided into sixty-six work groups. Within each work group the jobs are of the same general type and require similar capabilities and adaptabilities of workers. Capabilities include such factors as educational development, physical capacities, aptitudes, and job knowledge. Adaptabilities are necessary adjustments to work situations such as the work environment, routine, dealing with people, and working at set standards.

The guide provides a checklist of interest groups to complete. In each of the twelve interest areas, there is a general description of the type of work involved. The section gives detailed information about the activities of workers in the group, things about a person that indicate that he or she would be right for the kind of work described, skills and abilities that are needed to do the kind of work, and other facts one should consider about the work, such as the need for travel or continuing education. Examples of work groups include:

- Scientific: Physical sciences
                    Life sciences
                    Medical sciences
                    Laboratory technology

- Accommodating: Hospitality services
                    Barber and beauty services
                    Passenger services
                    Customer services
                    Attendant services

In addition to the general information and job titles, the guide provides codes for the *Dictionary of Occupational Titles (DOT)*. The DOT defines an occupation and the industry in which it can be found. The guide is helpful with both self-assessment and the world-of-work assessment that is mentioned later in the section.

Inventories

There are a number of other instruments available for use in determining your career interests. Two of the most popular include the *Strong Campbell Vocational Interest Inventory* and the *Harrington O'Shea Career Decision Making System*. These are administered by trained certified professionals in college and university, business, or counseling environments.

The *Strong Campbell Vocational Interest Inventory* is based on the work of John Holland. It identifies your level of interest in six major areas, known as the Holland Codes. They are realistic, investigative, artistic, social, enterprising and conventional.

The *Harrington O'Shea Career Decision Making System* is similar to the *Strong Campbell* in that it includes an interest inventory—however, it also requires that you identify occupational and educational preferences, work values, abilities, and future occupational plans. As with the *Strong Campbell Interest Inventory*, your interests are scored in six major areas. They are crafts, scientific, the arts, social, business, and clerical. These correspond to the six Holland codes.

The *Harrington O'Shea* is a more in-depth research tool, as it provides the structure to identify values, skills, educational requirements, and occupational preferences. The results of the interest inventory can be used, in conjunction with *The Guide For Occupational Exploration*, to identify over twenty thousand possible occupational titles for further investigation.

The following table demonstrates the relationship between the six *Strong Campbell* and the *Harrington O'Shea* interest scores and offers descriptions of interests and characteristics.

SC=Strong Campbell   HO=Harrington O'Shea

Realistic (SC) **Crafts (HO)**	Interested in practical mechanical activities that often call for physical strength. Prefers working with tools and objects rather than words and people. Desires practical results from work.
Investigative (SC) **Scientific (HO)**	Values mathematics and scientific work. Tends to be curious, creative, theoretical, and studious. Often prefers to work alone.
Artistic (SC) **The Arts (HO)**	Interested in creative activities, such as music, writing, entertainment, and art. Often prefers a nonconforming life-style, prizes independence, and actively searches out opportunities for self-expression.
Social (SC) **Social (HO)**	Interested in the well-being of others, gets along well with others, and has strong verbal skills.
Enterprising (SC) **Business (HO)**	Sees self as skilled with words. Attracted to careers that provide opportunities to lead others and to convince others to think the way he or she does or to buy his or her products.
Conventional (SC) **Clerical (HO)**	Prefers occupations in which the duties are clearly defined. Typically enjoys organized tasks and the verbal and numerical activities of office work. Tends to be orderly and systematic.

Based on your scores in the interest inventories, you will be able to identify typical occupations to explore and also be able to rate them in terms of their ability to meet your value system and utilize your abilities. Further work can be done using *The Guide for Occupational Exploration* discussed earlier in this section and the *Dictionary of Occupational Titles*. Both of these instruments are thorough and provide you with a list of concrete occupations based on your interest results.

There are other vocational and career decision-making instruments, such as the computerized SIGI-PLUS and Discover systems, which are available for self-assessment. SIGI-PLUS and Discover are interactive software programs that provide career, occupational, and educational information. The programs are easy to use and provide individualized assistance in learning about career needs and goals. Detailed information is available on hundreds of occupations. The Self Directed Search is a non-computerized, comprehensive self-assessment instrument, similar to SIGI-PLUS and Discover. Check with campus career counseling professionals or visit a college career center; private career counselors also offer them.

Soul searching   During your early years (age four to eighteen), you were exposed to many working people: parents, family members, and/or professionals in the workplace. Through radio and television, the written media, and life in general, role models were identified, opinions formed, and careers were envisioned.

Reflect back to your early years. Who were your heroes and mentors? Many children want to become police officers, fire fighters, lawyers, doctors, nurses, educators, scientists, truck drivers. Your interests form early in life.

Create a list of people who had an impact on you and think for a moment about why they were so attractive. You may have wanted to become a famous entertainer. Today you may think that dream was ridiculous, furthest from the realm of possibility. That is probably true. Now, go one step further. Why did you want to emulate a famous entertainer? Was it his or her public appeal, life style, or the image he or she projected? Identifying these factors may be helpful in providing clues to your career interests. It's possible that you may also want to work in an industry or career field where you will receive admiration, fame, or power, or you may want to find an occupation that offers public contact and requires leadership qualities. What occupations will meet the criteria of your childhood fantasy? What occupations will meet your current criteria? Once you have identified your fantasy career/role models, you can look at ways to identify information on careers that meet the same criteria.

Perfect day

Spend a few minutes jotting down a description of what you consider a perfect first career job. Do not place any restrictions on yourself at this time. Merely paint the perfect day.

- Where would you be geographically?
- How would you get to work? Car, bus, walk, train?
- What would your work environment be like? Office, travel, outdoors?
- Does your work involve people, data, or ideas?
- How much pay will you receive?
- What benefits will be provided?
- How large is the company?
- Are you in management?
- Do you work with equipment, on computers?
- Is the job physical, noisy, quiet?
- Are you paid on a commission basis, hourly, or salary?
- Would you be selling, creating, serving?

The answers to these questions will provide clues about career fields and occupations that will give you satisfaction.

Past work and volunteer history

The last exercise to complete in identifying your interests requires that you make a list of previous jobs and volunteer positions that you have held throughout your working life. After you generate your list, take a piece of paper for each position and write all of the activities that you performed while in each one. Don't stop and think about whether each activity was important, useful, difficult, worthy, or productive. Just write! Once you have written down all activities for the first position, start on the second one and go until you complete every one. Put the lists aside for a day or two and then go back to them and see if there is anything else that you can add.

Next, analyze the information and develop themes from your past experiences.

- Is there a theme that runs through your previous positions?
- Do they fall, for example, within the service industry?
- Did they require leadership skills?
- What interest patterns are you able to develop from your analysis?
- Is there a particular work function, industry, or sector (public, private, non-profit) of greater interest?

Now write down areas of interest that you have identified.

AREAS OF INTEREST

#1 _____

#2 _____

#3 _____

#4 _____

You have now seen how self-assessment exercises provide the structure through which you will be able to identify the type of information necessary for the career-planning and decision-making process. Almost everyone who does some form of self-assessment is left with useful information, especially about top skills, interests, and values. Some people going through the process find the answer to the question "What will I do in my career?" Many are so comfortable with the information that they take it and begin a job-search campaign, pursuing numerous career options and endless opportunities. Others freeze with anxiety, looking for concrete answers to the question of how to begin their career search.

Chances are that self-assessment will leave you more knowledgeable about yourself. It may also leave you frustrated and anxious about the need to develop methods to achieve your goals while utilizing your skills and interests and meeting your value system. At this point in the process don't get overly concerned about not having all the answers. You have the whole world of work available to you, with few limitations to hold you back. Use your own imagination and don't be afraid to explore new opportunities or meet new people. Reluctance to do so may hurt you more than any other single factor.

Be sure to save all the information that you generated in the self-assessment exercises for use later in the market analysis section.

Market Analysis

Having completed the values, skills, and interest exercises, you are ready to identify career fields and industries that will provide you with the opportunity to meet the criteria that you've deemed important to you. The reason consumer products companies are successful is that they do a great deal of research, find their market niche, and target strategies to penetrate that niche. You must do the same. Market analysis will provide insight into how you can learn more about the world of work and how you, the human product, can penetrate your special corner of this world.

If you are the type of person who needs structure and concrete job titles, then thorough market analysis is an extremely essential element in your planning process. By way of illustration, consider Marty, who is about to explore his career options.

Exploring Your Options

Marty will be graduating from a small college in New England with a degree in business studies and a concentration in marketing. Because he is concerned with his career development, he has completed self-assessment exercises in the hope of gaining a clearer picture of his values, skills, and interests. Marty prefers to remain in the New England area after graduation. Athletic activities are his favorite hobbies. Marty's top *values* are: job security, opportunity for leadership, geographic preference, variety, and the ability to earn a good salary. His *skills* are in the areas of sales, promotion, and public speaking. He also has excellent interpersonal skills. His *interests* are strong in business and athletics. It was clear that something in the sports management industry might be good for Marty. Through brainstorming he has developed a list of possible careers in the sporting industry and has came up with some options. In order to learn about all of the possible occupations in his areas of interest he is using *The Guide for Occupational Exploration*. He has also met with the athletic director at his college, who has assisted him in further identifying careers in the industry. He has looked at books written about careers in sports management, and he has met with the college director of public information, the manager of a professional sports team, and the director of the local YMCA. Through his research Marty has come up with a number of career options warranting further exploration. He has finally narrowed his options to three. They are health club manager, promotions manager for a professional sports team, and manufacturer's representative for an athletic equipment marketer. Marty has checked his skills, education, interest, abilities, and values against those needed in the three employment areas he is considering.

The first thing that Marty did in analyzing his potential markets was to look at the *Dictionary of Occupational Titles* so that he could get an accurate definition of the occupations that he was exploring. The DOT is a very useful resource, as it provides a brief description of an occupation, allowing the user to gather information and make a quick initial decision. Marty was pleased to find that the descriptions provided reinforced his desire for a career in sports management. The next step in Marty's planning process is *informational interviewing*, an excellent research tool in strategic self-marketing.

Informational interviewing

There is no better source of firsthand, up-to-date, realistic career information than people who are working in your field of interest. Most people are more than happy to answer any questions you might ask.

Make a list of people you already know who might provide information or become referrals. Start with friends, relatives, peers, faculty, work supervisors, or neighbors. Ask around! Also, try to recall speakers you have heard or people you have read about. Other resources include professional organizations, organization directories, and chambers of commerce. If you cannot obtain names of contacts in your field of interest, you can always call a trade organization and ask who is in charge of the particular department in question. Many college and university career centers maintain alumni data bases that can be very useful in providing informational interviewing contacts.

Most working people are flattered by requests from students or career changers for information and advice, and they are usually willing to help. It is up to you, however, to initiate the contact. This can be done by a "cold" telephone call, or by writing a letter and following it up with a phone call. Another method is to have someone who knows you make the appointment for you. If you were referred to your contact by someone, you might want to mention the name of your referral source when calling or writing to introduce yourself.

When arranging your interview, explain that your purpose is information gathering. You might say: "I'm a student at Jamesville College and I'm considering a career in _____. At the moment I'm researching the field and would very much like to meet with you to gather information and advice." Ask your contact for twenty minutes to half an hour of time at his or her convenience.

Be aware that support staff may try to discourage you by telling you that no jobs are available or that you should go immediately to the human resources person or department. It is important for you to be assertive at this point and clarify that you are seeking information, not a job. Some students or career changers have found it helpful to say that they are involved in career counseling and have been advised to speak to someone who works in their field of interest.

After all your hard work, you will probably be granted an interview. Before the appointment time, assess your interests, values, and skills. It is imperative that you be knowledgeable and able to discuss intelligently the reasons you have chosen to research this particular field. You should also read all you can about the field prior to conducting the interview.

Dress neatly for the interview. Handle yourself in a professional manner. Make sure that you are on time. Try to establish good rapport with your contact and indicate an interest in his or her career. Refer to your list of prepared questions (see below), but allow the discussion some spontaneity as well. The final question you should ask is "If you were in my place whom would you suggest I talk to next?"

After the interview, be sure to record the name, address, and phone number of the contact, all of which can be obtained from his or her business card. Also note the date of the interview, the information gathered, and the names of additional referrals. Within a week of the interview, you should send a thank-you note to the person with whom you interviewed.

Remember, when evaluating a career choice, to differentiate between your interest in the career and the impression the person you interviewed made on you. Often a great interview with a likeable person can affect your decision making. It should be what he or she says about the field that becomes the input into your planning process, not the personality of the interviewee.

If in the future you decide to pursue a career or seek employment as a result of an informational interview, a letter notifying the person you interviewed would be in order. You may also want to send a cover letter and resume to this same person when you begin your job search.

And now, back to Marty. His informational interviewing completed, he begins to sense that, as a new college graduate, all three positions are realistic options for him. The next step is to explore existing opportunities.

Sample questions that you may ask during an informational interview

1. How did you get involved in this line of work?
2. In the position you now hold, what do you do on a typical day?
3. What do you find most interesting about your job?
4. Is your work ever boring or repetitive?
5. What was your prior experience?
6. What is your next logical career move?
7. What is the top job you aspire to in this career field?
8. What are the transfer possibilities in this field?
9. Would you suggest specific courses of study that would be particularly beneficial for success in this field?
10. What are the basic prerequisites for jobs in this field?

11. What experiences qualify one for this field?

12. What types of training do companies offer professionals in this field?

13. What are the salary ranges for various levels in this field?

14. What aspects of a career in this field do you consider particularly good?

15. What special advice would you give to a young person entering this field?

16. Is there a demand for people in this field?

17. What type of change do you anticipate occurring in the next five to ten years?

18. What is the best way to start a career in this field?

19. May I read job descriptions and specifications for some of the positions in this field?

20. What periodicals do you subscribe to?

21. What professional memberships do you hold?

Through the informational interview process, Marty already has begun to get a sense of the "health" of different industries. Health club managers are in high demand. Sports team promotions management positions are competitive, and although available, one has to dig for manufacturer's representative jobs since they are rarely advertised.

Since Marty's informational interviewing contacts referred him to other professionals in the field, he made more appointments and furthered his research. He ended up with a list of eight names to contact. Six of the eight agreed to see him for the purpose of providing information. One of the final two canceled, but the last person gave him the name of someone else in the company who would be an excellent contact.

Marty did not rely solely on informational interviewing to gather data on the three career fields he was researching. He utilized the public and college libraries and the resources of the college career center to gather additional information.

When Marty completed exploring his career options he developed the following table. This was helpful to him as he pulled together his self-assessment and market analysis information. The table shows how his interests, skills, and values results relate to the occupations he identified as possible choices in his market analysis. The X's indicate a match.

Table of Self-Assessment/Occupations Match

OCCUPATIONS	Health Club Manager	Promotions Manager	Manufacturer's Representative
Interests			
sports	_____x_____	_____x_____	_____x_____
business	_____x_____	_____x_____	_____x_____
_____	_____	_____	_____
_____	_____	_____	_____
Values			
security	_____x_____	_____	_____
leadership	_____x_____	_____x_____	_____
geographic	_____?_____	_____?_____	_____?_____
variety	_____x_____	_____x_____	_____x_____
salary	_____?_____	_____x_____	_____x_____
Skills			
sales/promo	_____x_____	_____x_____	_____x_____
public speaking	_____	_____x_____	_____x_____
rapport	_____x_____	_____x_____	_____x_____
_____	_____	_____	_____

Once your self-assessment and market analysis are complete, you can start to develop yourself as a marketable product. Self-assessment has allowed you to analyze your skills, and market assessment has given you the information to match those skills to available jobs that interest you and fit your value system. The planning stage is vitally important, for a good marketing mix cannot be developed without research.

The Guide For Occupational Exploration is another resource for gathering general information about the world of work. The information available in the guide is divided into sections.

- *General description* of the kind of people in each group, where they work, and what they do.

- *The kind of work you would like to do* features typical job activities.

- *Things about yourself that point to this kind of work* identifies the work values held strongly by members of the work group, preferred leisure activities, favorite school subjects, physical capabilities, and the settings where jobs are located.

- *Skills and abilities needed for this kind of work* includes physical and mental abilities necessary to succeed in this work.

- *Things you should consider about this kind of work* includes need for travel, evening or overtime work, continuing education, or special location.

- *How you can prepare for most jobs* provides information on the level of education or training usually required in addition to lists of helpful courses.

- *Licenses and certificates* lists any occupations that require licenses or certificates, including the license or certificate that is required.

- *Organizations and agencies to contact* lists government agencies, professional organizations, and publishing companies that offer information about jobs.

The planning stage of your strategic self-marketing plan is complete after you have done a thorough self-assessment and completed as thorough a market analysis as possible. Once these two projects are finished, you can begin to develop your self-marketing mix.

Business and
Occupation Information
Resources

The following publications will help you find the information you need to do a competent market analysis. Check your university or public library.

American Almanac of Jobs and Salaries by John Wright. Avon Books, 1988.

Annual Corporate Reports.

Career Choice Encyclopedia. Walker and Company, 1986.

Career Guide—Dun's Employment Opportunities Directory. Published annually.

Career Press Directory Series by Ronald Fry. Career Press Inc.
    Advertising Career Directory. 3rd Edition, 1988.
    Business and Finance Career Directory. 1st Edition, 1989.
    Marketing and Sales Directory. 2nd Edition, 1988.
    Public Relations Career Directory. 2nd Edition, 1988.
    Travel Industry Career Directory. 1st Edition, 1989.

Chamber of Commerce Directories.

College Placement Council National Directory. Vols. 1–4, published annually.

Corporate Directory. Gale Research Inc., 1990.

Dictionary of Occupational Titles. U.S. Department of Labor, 1977 (latest edition).

Directory of Directories by James Ethridge and Cecelia Ann Marlow. Information Enterprises, published biennially. Distributed by Gale Research.

Directory of American Firms Operating in Foreign Countries. World Trade Academy Press, 1987.

Directory of Manufacturers. Commerce Register, published annually.

Dun and Bradstreet Million Dollar Directory. Dun's Marketing Services, published annually.

Dun's Marketing Services, published annually.

Encyclopedia of Associations. Gale Research Co., 1989.

Financial World America's Top Growth Companies Directory Issue. Financial World Partners, published annually.

Forbes Up-and-Comers 200: Best Small Companies in America. Forbes, Inc., published annually.

Fortune Directory. Time, Inc., published annually.

Good Works by Joan Anzalone. Red Dembner Enterprises Corp., 1985.

Industry Trade Journals.

International Directories of American Companies Abroad. International Publications, 1989.

The Job Bank Series. Bob Adams Inc., published annually.

MacMillan Directory of Leading Private Companies. National Register Publishing Company, published annually.

MacRaes Blue Book. Business Research Publications, Inc., published annually.

Manufacturing USA: Industry Analyses, Statistics, and Leading Companies. Gale Research Co., 1989.

Network of Small Business Membership Directory. NSB, 1989.

National Trade and Professional Associations of the United States by Craig Colgate, Jr. Columbia Books, 1987.

100 Best Companies to Work for. Signet, Penguin Books, 1985.

Peterson's Guides. Peterson's Guides, published annually.

Principal International Directory. Dun and Bradstreet, 1991.

Standard and Poor's Register of Corporations, Directors and Executives. Standard and Poor's Corp., published annually.

Standard Periodical Directory. Oxbridge Publishing Co., biennial.

U.S. Bureau of Labor Statistics, *Occupational Outlook Handbook.* U.S. Department of Labor, 1991.

U.S. Bureau of Labor Statistics, *Occupational Outlook Quarterly.* U.S. Department of Labor, published quarterly.

U.S. Private Companies. Information Access Co., published annually.

VGM Career Horizon Series. VGM Career Horizons, various publication dates.

Wall Street Journal. Published daily.

THE HUMAN PRODUCT

Section III

Kevin Joyce,
Manager of Executive Recruitment and
College Relations, Filenes

Each year, America's colleges and universities are turning out numerous well-educated graduates seeking opportunities to enhance their skills in the workplace. For some, this is a challenging time to meet prospective employers, accept invitations for site visits, and subsequently choose the right company with which to begin their first professional work experience. For others, many of whom are equally qualified, this becomes a lengthier and sometimes frustrating endeavor.

When entry-level opportunities are fewer, it is extremely important for a candidate to present to an employer the most attractive package of qualifications possible. Seizing the competitive edge is an endeavor involving significant prework. Honest self-assessment, meticulous resume preparation, careful company research, and practiced interview skills together provide opportunities for candidates to grasp this advantage. Poised, articulate, and appropriately dressed prospects will almost always out-compete those individuals who bypass these critical steps.

Just as a "great new product" is launched in the consumer market with an aggressive campaign, so too should a bright and eager graduate develop a similar strategy to command the attention of the targeted market.

Self-Product Development and Positioning

Developing yourself as the "ideal" candidate for success, both during the job search and on the job, requires that special attention be paid to the controllable variables—personality, skills, interests, education, and image—that are the component parts of all human products.

Self-Product Mix Components

Personality. The formal definition of personality is a set of enduring traits or characteristics that distinguish one individual from another. Employers consistently mention personality traits such as enthusiasm and initiative as being important in the candidates they consider for employment. If you do not already possess these two traits, develop them. They are strengths you can capitalize on as you progress through the job search and throughout your career. Not having them does not mean that you will be overlooked. It is in your best interest, however, to be aware of what employers consider to be important.

Skills. Skill identification and development was already discussed at length earlier, but it should be mentioned again. Since ideal candidates must possess the skills necessary to perform the functions of the job from day one, those skills are important elements in self-product development.

It is possible, through study and practice, to hone the skills you already possess to perfection, but it is not possible to perfect skills that are outside of your mental or physical abilities. For example, a ninety-pound man or woman cannot become a dockworker if the job requires lifting hundred-pound-plus containers on a regular basis. A person who is color blind cannot become a fashion coordinator if color coordination of various fashion items is an integral part of the job. Someone with poor mechanical coordination and who has a problem understanding computer technology should not attempt to become a computer engineer. Success can be yours if you concentrate on those skills that can be developed. Don't waste time on those that cannot.

Interests. Ideal candidates express their interest for a position or field through a discussion of prior achievements and activities, both on resumes and during interviews. You cannot expect an employer to hire you strictly on your "expression" of interest. You should be ready to identify the link between your past experiences and interests and future aspirations. Because it is much too costly for employers to lose new staff through attrition, they will not generally take risks without a proven interest history.

To develop this history, start recording your interests, even prior to your job search. Take an interest inventory to determine if your interests match your skills. Discuss your areas of interest with people you know whose interests are similar to yours and who are employed in industries or in jobs that have always seemed ideal to you. As you go through this process, you will begin to target and develop those specific interests that will give you that proven history necessary to impress potential employers.

Education. A college degree continues to increase in value. It is actually a necessity for those looking for professional employment and movement up the career ladder. A quick browse through the professional section of the want ads will demonstrate the need for and importance of a college degree. If you are looking for a skill-specific position, such as accounting, nursing, or engineering, then a technical degree will most likely be required for consideration by potential employers. For nontechnical professions such as those in sales or management, either a business or liberal arts degree is required. Does this mean that you won't find work or climb the corporate ladder without a degree? Not necessarily, but trends show that degrees are being required by more and more employers each year.

Be sure you investigate the educational requirements in your chosen career field. If you research these prior to selecting your major course of study, you can more easily guarantee this component of your product mix. What happens, however, if halfway through your educational preparation you decide that you are headed in the wrong direction? Not to worry! Educational preparation and skills are transferable. Thinking, writing, speaking, and decision making, the most important elements developed during any education, will serve you well, whatever direction you take.

Image. Image is a critical variable in self-product development. Judgments are made on the image you project and its match with the image of the company where you are seeking employment. From the first time you communicate with an employer, either in writing or in person, your image is on display.

Most often, first impressions are conveyed through letters and/or resumes. Imagine yourself as the human resources director of a large corporation who receives a letter of application, written on orchid stationery. The writer—let's say it's a man—has one strike against him, even before the envelope is opened. The letter (on matching paper, of course) has a number of grammatical errors. Strike two. By the time the resume emerges from behind the letter, the applicant has already made a somewhat negative impression, so when the reader sees a crossed-out address with the correct one handwritten beside it, it's strike three and you're out!

Now this might be an extreme example of how an employer receives a negative image from a job applicant, but it does point out the reality of first impressions and why they are such important components of image development. If we assume that the "orchid" applicant had excellent skills, a good educational background, and sufficient experience to be considered a potential candidate for the opening in our fictitious corporation, it's unfortunate that he spent so little time learning how to convey a positive self-image on paper. The steps to proper letter and resume writing, so important in image development, will be discussed in later chapters.

Prior to putting together an effective resume, you should complete the self-assessment exercise and the world-of-work exploration referred to earlier. With these in mind and the information on letters and resumes still to come on future pages, you will never fall into the same trap as our "orchid applicant," and therefore you will get the interview or interviews you want. During an interview, you should display, in person, the type of positive image that says to an employer, "I am the person you want for the job. I understand your company's culture and how and where I fit."

Self-packaging   The key to successful self-presentation is personal packaging. Your self-package consists of (1) your appearance; (2) your personal mannerisms, including the way you walk, the way you sit, and the way you speak; and (3) your personal hygiene habits. If even one of these aspects of your personal package is negative, it can taint your total image. Consider each one carefully when putting yourself together. Certain rules are universal and deviations are not allowed, except in rare instances when, for example, wild, tricolored hair—one of the "no-no's" of proper packaging for success—might be the factor that gets you an audition with a hard rock band.

The universal rules just mentioned are as follows:

1. Keep yourself healthy and fit.

2. Always be sure your breath is fresh.

3. Never chew gum in any professional setting.

4. Always have clean, conservatively styled hair.

5. Always use deodorant.

6. Always be sure your clothes are clean, pressed, and odor free.

7. Always be sure your nails are clean and well trimmed. Women, no long red claws; save that look for Halloween parties.

8. Never smoke during a job interview or at a business lunch, even if the interviewer offers you a cigarette.

9. Never order an alcoholic beverage if interviewed at lunch or dinner, even if the interviewer is drinking. Remember, you must be in complete control of all you say and do.

Appearance. Don't let anyone ever tell you that your personal appearance during the interview process is unimportant or secondary to other self-product components. First impressions stick, and it is much more difficult to undo a bad impression than it is to make a special effort to put your best self forward first time around. *You will never get a second chance to make a first impression; make the most of number one!*

Exactly how does one make this all-important first impression? Well, it isn't style, elegance, or wearing the very latest look from *Glamour* or *Gentleman's Quarterly*; rather, it is the ability to wear clothes with confidence, to know that what you have selected as your "interview outfit" is current, professional, well-tailored to your body and proves to the interviewer that you are compatible with the employer's expectations. All clothes make a statement about the wearer. Professional clothes should make a background statement and not distract from your total image.

Although you should not dress for an interview as you would for a social occasion, neither should you dress in "uniform." Women may wear an appropriate but distinctive blouse and should not imitate their male competitors with a shirt and tie. Even a small string tie could say to the interviewer, "I can handle this job like a man." You are not a man, so why pretend! Men, of course, are best in navy or gray suits with white or light blue shirts. Ties are usually of the striped variety, picking up the color of the suit. Wear matching knee-high executive socks. Bare legs above short socks are hardly appealing. There is nothing wrong with a solid red tie if your suit is navy and your shirt is white. You must, however, feel comfortable in a red tie in order to wear it with ease.

Study the Business Basics Chart for men and women. It is a pretty good personal appearance guide; no matter where you live or the level of job you're interviewing for, the same basic principles apply. Your clothing, like your demeanor, should be unstudied and provide the proper background. You want to be remembered for yourself, not for your suit or jewelry.

BUSINESS BASICS*

WOMEN

- Tailored clothing only. Avoid frills, ruffles, plunging necklines, and polyester.

- Suits and blazers in plain, neutral colors or understated plaids or checks. Select colors that go with your skin tones and hair color.

- Dresses in solid colors, worn with or without blazers.

- Scarves for color accents, if you look good in scarves and know how to use them.

- Skirts that are pleated, straight or dirndl, with no extreme slits; not too long or too short. The best length is just at the knee, unless you feel the need to cover more of your leg. If you do, be sure the length is in proportion to your jacket (if a suit) and shoes.

- Basic dark pumps with medium heels that match your outfit. Avoid six-inch heels and sling backs.

- A simple dress watch. Stud earrings in gold or pearl. Avoid dangling bracelets. Never wear more than two at one time. One ring on each hand is the maximum.

- Flesh tone stockings. Avoid textures and patterns. Wear black or navy or gray as an extension of a black, navy, or gray suit and *only* if very, very light in tone.

- Light perfume only.

- A tailored handbag and/or briefcase. It is not necessary to carry both.

MEN

- Navy or gray, wool or light-weight wool blend suits, solid, pinstriped, or shadow plaid. Navy blazer and gray trousers is an acceptable alternative. No polyester.

- Suit lapels should be no wider than your necktie.

- Dress shirts in solid colors, mostly white, pale blue, or yellow. Never wear a shirt with a frayed collar.

- Ties in muted colors and in contrast to the suit. Solids, stripes, or small patterns.

- Calf-length hose in dark colors to match suit.

- Black or brown 1-inch belt.

- Tassel loafers, wing-tips, or laced-up shoes.

- Avoid flashy cuff-links, rings, or neck chains.

- A simple dress watch is best.

- Avoid a strong aftershave or cologne.

*Variations depend upon industry, job type, and geography. Interview preparation should always include research into the exact image desired in each setting.

Assistance in selecting your professional wardrobe is available from retailers who sell business attire. Work with a salesperson with whom you feel comfortable when purchasing your interviewing outfit. Don't be afraid to ask questions concerning current fashion, but do not be swayed by the salesperson's concern with "the latest" or "a new hot item." Avoid approaching any sales employee whose own appearance is drastically opposed to the professional image you are seeking.

Mannerisms. Your mannerisms are expressed through the four "S's": the way you *stand, sit, shake hands,* and *speak.*

The first time most interviewers see prospective job candidates is when they are standing in front of them. Walk tall as you enter the interview room, regardless of your height. Tall people tend to slouch, and shorter people often do not pull themselves up to their full potential. Your posture says a great deal about your self-image. A 4′11″ woman can appear taller if she keeps her head up, shoulders straight, walks and stands with confidence, and shakes hands firmly. A 6′2″ man can appear weak and without confidence if he slouches when he stands and shakes hands limply. *Always* look the interviewer straight in the eye when shaking hands and throughout the interview.

Sit down when requested. If the interviewer should forget to ask you to sit, it is perfectly permissible to ask, "May I sit down?" The way you sit can also reveal a great deal about your self-confidence. Stand tall and sit tall, but not so that you appear unrelaxed. Do not lean back and cross your legs at the knees. This is especially true for women. Keeping your hands folded in your lap, one on top of the other, palms up, will stop you from engaging in unwanted nervous gestures. Sometimes, sitting at a slight angle instead of straight, presents a good image. Above all, sit so that you are comfortable. It's stressful enough to answer an interviewer's questions without worrying about how you look as you do this.

The most important "S" of all is the way you speak. Proper English usage is a must. All employers look for employees who are articulate and can express themselves easily and correctly. *Never* use slang. Your English professors were right about the necessity for good verbal expression and a well-modulated voice. Study and practice. Take a course in public speaking or just keep talking to someone who you consider to be a "speech" role model. The great first impression you made as you sat down for your interview will die if the first words out of your mouth are phony, stupid, or pronounced incorrectly. Above all else, find out the correct pronunciation of your interviewer's name before, not after, the initial meeting.

Personal Hygiene. The universal rules stated at the beginning of this section cover most of the important aspects of personal hygiene. The perfume/aftershave question is addressed in the Business Basics Chart on page 56. Pay strict attention to both as you develop your self-image.

Positioning Yourself for Success

It is imperative that you keep the competition in perspective during your job search. If you are still in college, look around and study your peers who will be graduating with you and are interested in the same career field. Each of them can be potential competitors for those jobs you are seeking. Expand your peer pool mentally so that it includes all college graduates in your state or, for that matter, in any state, and you will see that there is a very large pool of candidates from which employers may choose. Some competitors may be looking at different industries than the ones that interest you; therefore, they do not all represent direct competition. Career changers, one or many years out of college, are another source of competition, both for about-to-be-graduates and for each other. In a tight job market, studying the competition is especially important if you are to position yourself properly for the interviews and employment opportunities.

As you climb the career ladder, the competition becomes greater as the jobs become fewer. Your task is to place yourself properly against your competition with the goal of achieving success in your job search, at whatever point in your life it is occurring. Proper positioning means putting yourself in the right place at the right time so that you will be noticed. Even if you graduated from a small, private Midwestern college and the large corporation that represents your "dream" employer only recruits at Ivy League institutions, you still have a chance at employment. All large corporations' new hires, regardless of where the corporations recruit, do not come exclusively from the Ivys; some new employees enter through the internship door or are interviewed because of the recommendation of a current employee who is a friend of the prospect's family and knows that he or she is worth interviewing. Effective networking, an unsolicited eye-catching resume, internships, or cooperative education experiences can all help bring you to the attention of the potential employers of your choice, even when the sheer number of competitors seems overwhelming.

In retailing, there is a basic principle that says if you have the right merchandise in the right place at the right time and at the right price, it will sell. This same principle can apply to you, the human product, as long as you have developed yourself into the right product and can position or place yourself against the competition at a time and place that gives you an edge. If you want to start working in California in September and are still doing a long distance preliminary search from Montana in July, your chances of finding what you want at the time you want it and in the place you want it are not as good as someone with your same qualifications who has positioned himself or herself in California (moved west from New Jersey in May) and is available for interviews with less than a day's notice. Even if you are the better candidate, you could come in second, third, or fourth. Being in the right place at the right time counts!

The best product in the world will not "sell" if the customer finds the purchase process too difficult or too lengthy, nor will it sell if no one knows about it. Position yourself for success against the competition through (1) networking, (2) extensive mailing of unsolicited resumes to employers of your choice, and (3) physical access. You will only be considered over others if you stand out in the crowd.

The Human Product Life Cycle

5

Stages of the Cycle   The four stages of the human product life cycle, like all product life cycles, are *introduction, growth, maturity,* and *decline.* Not everyone will go through each of the stages in his or her working life. But it is important to understand the basic differences of every stage since there are changes that typify each one. The material here will focus primarily on the introductory stage, where you begin as a new college graduate to market and utilize your college degree.

Introductory stage   This first stage, where you introduce yourself to potential purchasers, is characterized by high energy, a strong desire to succeed, and a determination to learn. It symbolizes independence and signifies adulthood. During the introductory stage, your work and your occupation become the major focus of your life. The concept of career will begin to take on meaning as you take stock of where your education and life have brought you and you begin to look forward to where you would like to be in five years. At this phase you explore the possibilities of your first job and, with your first employers, test some initial choices, build your first professional image, and participate in teamwork.

Growth stage

This stage is achieved when the concept of career is tied in with the notion of growth in your current position or acknowledgment that there is a substantive connection between one job and the next one that follows. Skill development, further education, salary increases, and promotions are values you should seek during this stage.

Maturity stage

Stage III is characterized by prominence in your career position. You should have achieved self-esteem by this time or, in worst case scenarios, reached a dead end. If your working life has been successful, you may achieve self-actualization, either within one company or with many employers. Self-actualization is the ultimate goal in human development. It means that you have maximized your interests, values, and skills to a point where you are totally satisfied in your professional life and usually, as a result, in your personal life as well.

Decline stage

The decline stage is characterized by stagnation and decline from previous levels of career success. If, however, you continue to work on yourself, improving and changing the "product," as needed, during each of the first three stages of your human product life cycle, you will not have to face decline. The following examples will help you to understand better the human product life cycle.

Two Career Stories

Stage I—Introduction. Sarah and Bill are new college graduates. Sarah is twenty-one years old and was a full-time day school student at the same college where Bill, thirty-four, attended nights. Both are accounting majors and are hired at graduation by the same CPA firm, through the on-campus recruiting program. They start to climb the career ladder at the same time.

During the first year on the job both Sarah and Bill work extremely hard. They are energized by the work, their environment, interaction with clients, and the opportunity to use their education in a productive way, both for themselves and their employer. Bill begins to study for the CPA exam. Sarah decides to wait another year to begin her preparation. Bill and Sarah are receiving the same yearly salary and benefits. They are satisfied with their compensation because they know it is standard for first year employees in their profession.

As the months pass, the need to work overtime becomes apparent. Never a clock watcher, Bill is often found at his desk long after five p.m. Sarah, on the other hand, is willing to put in extra time, but since professional accountants do not expect or receive additional pay for additional hours, she only does this when it is absolutely necessary. Clients seem to like Bill and Sarah, and both receive very good six month evaluations. Sarah relates especially well to small-business people and, much to the delight of her employer, has the uncanny ability to understand their financial problems without too much explanation. Bill would rather deal with corporate clients and does this more and more as the managing partner begins to recognize his expertise in this area.

Year one fades into year two and before they realize it, Bill and Sarah are beginning their third year with the firm. Both have received more than one raise and both have their own clients, no longer depending upon assignments from the client pool. Bill has passed his CPA exam. Sarah has not yet taken it, though she has completed her preparation.

Stage II—Growth. At the end of his third year, Bill is made a partner. At the end of her third year, Sarah decides to leave the firm and take a job as a comptroller in a very successful small company that manufactures computer software. Thus, both Bill and Sarah have moved from Stage I to Stage II. Bill has grown in his present firm and has moved from a trainee to a full-fledged partner. Sarah has taken the training and connections made while in her first position and used them to grow in a different direction. The important fact is that both Bill and Sarah are moving successfully through the first two stages of their working life cycle.

Stage III—Maturity. Based on Bill and Sarah's ability to grow and change as seen in Stages I and II, we will assume that the rest of their story is positive. Both Bill and Sarah reach prominence as they mature. After ten years, Bill becomes a managing partner of his firm, and Sarah is named outstanding businesswoman of the year in her community, two years in a row.

Stage IV—Decline. There will obviously be no decline for either Sarah or Bill. Retirement, yes, but only after they both achieve the life's success they wanted when they started on their life cycle so many years before. If either Bill or Sarah had been less ambitious or less dedicated, their life cycle could have ended in decline and obsolescence—two people who had the basics but never used them to climb beyond the first rung of the career ladder.

If you think of yourself as a product, develop a self-marketing plan, and engage in self-marketing strategies, your life cycle, like Sarah and Bill's, will never decline.

SELF-PROMOTION

Section IV

Jill A. Shea,
College Relations Coordinator
GTE Government Systems,
Command, Control & Communications

The purpose of the resume is to market your skill set. A well-written resume will usually secure an interview. Once an interview is confirmed, your personality plays an important role.

When putting a resume together, keep in mind that your resume should be unique to you. Recount your education, experiences, goals, and objectives. Then, relate them to the position for which you are applying.

If your college degree is newly acquired, list your education before work experience. Include your degree, major, minor, grade point average, and school attended, with month and year of graduation. List special interest courses, especially those directly related to the job you are seeking.

It is not necessary to include an objective unless you are specific in the job you are seeking. For example, if you are a chemical engineer and want to do research on chemical durability, then an objective would serve the purpose. However, many employers offer on-the-job training in areas such as sales or marketing, and for most recent graduates, some employers have a pool of entry-level opportunities. In either case, employers are seeking applicants with similar interests and aptitudes. Avoid vague or too general objectives. Elaborate on your education, skills, activities, and experiences. As stated, your resume should portray a bright person with relevant interests and aptitudes.

In writing your resume, use key words to focus on the similarities between yourself and the job. Key words reassure employers that you are compatible to their needs. For example, if you are seeking a financial position, words such as *cost estimating, analysis, lease, spreadsheet, investment,* and *auditors* could be used. Include action words. Avoid the use of first person. For example, you could use such phrases as "controlled cash flow," "served as a treasury liaison," and "evaluated forecasting."

Format the resume to highlight the commonality of your skills to the requirements of the job. Keep in mind that employers receive many resumes; therefore, unless the resume is properly formatted, the employer may not read it thoroughly.

Overall, credit yourself for previous work experience as well as outside activities. Remember, the resume is a summary of your professional history that includes the skills necessary to do the job. Your resume should not include a picture, your age, height, sex, race, or marital status, nor your religious or political affiliation.

Networking

Although selling oneself is a preliminary tactic in selling all goods and services, it is a major task in self-promotion. As mentioned earlier, there are three tactics that should be used when "getting the word out"—networking, the resume and cover letter, and the interview. Since you can control all three, use them well and success can be yours.

Networking as a concept has been in place for many years, but only recently has networking gained recognition from career counselors and career-planning professionals. According to recent workshop participants, more individuals are successful in obtaining job interviews through networking techniques than through any other method of job searching.

Networking or self-promotion is not new. The "old boy network," which has existed for years, is now just the "old network" since women have finally made it into the inner circles of business. With the number of women in the work force outnumbering men it seems likely that the "old girl network" may even become the network of the future.

Networking is a self-promotion process. It involves telling others that you are looking for employment. These contacts can then help to identify potential employers and can help you to learn about openings that may be of interest to you. Your contacts can include immediate family, extended family, friends, college affiliates, previous employment contacts, professional colleagues, and community members. All of these contacts have their own set of contacts. If they are aware of your desire for a job, they will remember you, if they hear of a position.

There was an old commercial that said if you told two friends about a new product and they told two friends who in turn told two other friends, before you knew it there would be a large number of people who were aware of the new item and would be looking for it in the stores. The same principle applies to someone who is searching for a job. Networking will help you "get the word out" to as many people as possible so that they can tell others, who will tell others etc, etc, etc.

The current employment market has led to the formation of many networking clubs. Their purpose is twofold; members help each other find jobs, and they provide support during periods of unemployment. It is an interesting phenomenon and very successful. It has also been proven that when individuals are referred to an employer, they are perceived differently than if they merely reply to an ad or make a cold call.

Networking bonds individuals together, as in the old story about a young boy trying to move a large boulder in his yard. His father, watching from inside their house and seeing that his son was becoming annoyed, went outside and asked his son if he was all right. The son replied, "No, I cannot move the boulder in spite of trying everything I know." His father told him that he hadn't tried everything and made a suggestion that might help him reach success in his mission. His suggestion? "Ask me for help. The two of us can surely move it." The son asked and the boulder was moved. The moral here is to ask for help if you need it. You can't do everything by yourself.

Networking Exercise

Develop your own networking list. Start by selecting twenty people you can network with as you begin your job search.

Your networking base:

1. _____

2. _____

3. _____

4. _____

5. _____

6. _____

7. _____

8. _____

9. _____

10. _____

11. _____

12. _____

13. _____

14. _____

15. _____

16. _____

17. _____

18. _____

19. _____

20. _____

It is important to network long before the date that you have set to begin working. Don't wait until you are ready for employment, as it takes time to cultivate and develop a networking base. Remember to follow up with your contacts on a regular basis. A critical aspect of networking is familiarization. People must remember who you are, and in the course of daily life, it is often easy for them to forget about your employment needs. Call periodically and remind them.

Some people cannot ask others for help. They are embarrassed or too proud. Erase those thoughts and feelings and accept the networking offers. The day may come when you can return the favor.

Networking vs. Informational Interviewing

There is a difference between networking and informational interviewing. If you know what you want in a particular industry, you can use networking. If you need more information about potential jobs or career paths, informational interviewing is the vehicle for you. Businesspeople know the difference between the two and may not appreciate your asking to see them for information if, in fact, you are looking for a job. If you are interviewing for information be sure that gaining information, not a job, is your real priority. There is no quicker way to distance yourself from potential employers and lose their trust in you than to arrive for an informational interview with a resume in your hand.

When networking, approach employers with confidence. Promote yourself by letting them know exactly what you are looking for and show how you can help them. If you leave a positive impression they will remember you if they have a position to fill in the future.

Considering that it is the number-one successful method for finding jobs and is also inexpensive, networking is certainly worth a try. Networking is not begging; rather, it is a respectable method of self-promotion.

When you are asked to interview or you receive a job offer, be sure to let your contact know. He or she will appreciate the feedback and a "thank you."

Even in a tight market, employers are not always able to meet all their employment needs through traditional methods. By networking you will be able to tap into the "hidden job market."

Another positive aspect of networking is that some of the elements of risk that exist for an employer in the hiring process are eliminated with referrals. Employers like the odds. Remember, networking may get you an interview, but only your performance during the interview will get you the job.

Networking in Action

Chad, who recently graduated from college with a degree in communications, had his heart set on working in advertising. While he was in school he completed an internship in the public relations department of Playboy Inc. in New York City. This reinforced his dream, and as a result, he was willing to work as hard as he could in order to climb the ladder in his chosen field. While working as a waiter, Chad networked continuously in hopes of uncovering an advertising job.

During his last semester in college, Chad had done informational interviewing with many advertising professionals. He learned a great deal from these interviews. After college, he turned his energy from informational interviewing to networking as a means of making contact with potential employers.

Within a few months after graduation, he was offered a twelve-week internship opportunity with a small agency outside of Boston, Massachusetts. He accepted because he felt that during the twelve-week program he could further develop his skills, enhance his resume, and meet more advertising professionals. He continued to network, asking each contact, "If you were me, who would you talk to next?" Two months after he completed his internship he received a phone call from a woman in one of the agencies he had visited while networking. She asked him if he was still looking for a job and then told him that there was an opening in her firm. He was interested and told her so. She set up an appointment for an interview with the senior manager of the firm.

Prior to the interview, Chad spoke with his agency contact to find out as many particulars about the position and organization as he could. The information he gained came in handy during the interview. Because his contact wanted Chad to look good, she gave him as much information as possible.

Chad and seven other candidates interviewed for the job. Within a week's time he was offered a position as account executive. The agency was one of the major advertising firms in Boston.

Chad was offered the position because of his attitude, professionalism, and knowledge. Without a referral, however, he might never have had the chance to know of the opening or to prove himself. It was the referral that got him the interview and eventually the job offer. He would not have been aware of the position had he not networked, for the position was never advertised. By using this important self-promotion tactic he gained the job of his dreams.

Of course, Chad had a good resume and excellent interviewing skills, the other two prongs that complete the three-pronged tactic known as self-promotion.

Even with the best resume and interpersonal skills in the world, you may not get the position you want if the right people do not know about you. Promote yourself through networking!

Resume and Cover Letter

The second prong in the three-pronged self-promotion tactic has two parts, the resume and the cover letter. First, the resume.

Tips for Creating Resumes

There are many views on how to use a resume in the job-search process. Traditionalists like Richard Bolles recognize their importance. Jack Falvey and others opt for getting rid of the resume altogether, and suggest relying on networking as the main method of self-promotion. Employers looking at new college graduates or career changers for professional positions will require a resume at some point in the recruiting process; it is inevitable. Proper packaging and distribution of your resume therefore is a most important self-promotion tool.

Earlier you were introduced to the importance of planning: identifying your skills, interests, and values. Prior to putting together an effective resume you should complete the self-assessment exercises and the world-of-work exploration. Through research you will gain a better sense of the career fields in which you will be seeking employment. Once you have completed these exercises you are ready to construct a resume.

For many, resume writing is perceived as a painful experience. As a result, career consultants and outplacement firms earn large amounts of money assisting job searchers create these promotional tools. Understanding how your resume will be viewed from a prospective employer's viewpoint will help to clear up some of the mystery surrounding this document and its use and make the process a little less painful.

Resumes are personal marketing tools. They are essential in the job search, and they can make the difference between getting the job or not getting the job. In many cases a linear progression occurs during the process. You submit a resume and cover letter in response to an advertisement, referral, or job fair contact. If the resume indicates that you are the person the employer is seeking, you will probably get an interview. If this goes well, you may even receive a job offer. Of course, the process is not as simple as it sounds here since there are many other factors, both controllable and uncontrollable, to be considered.

Your resume needs to tell an employer who you are, what you have done, and what you know. Most important, however, it must indicate what you have to offer. If you have completed the self-assessment outlined earlier, you will have a much easier time putting an effective resume together; if not, it will probably be more difficult.

Begin the construction of your resume with a thorough outline of your background. Brainstorm on your own or with family and friends to generate information on your educational, work, and personal experiences. Your educational experience includes your schools, degrees, majors, courses, seminars, research projects, papers, and honors. Your work experience includes both full- and part-time work, volunteering, co-operative education experiences or internships, field work, and class projects. Your personal information includes activities, interests, clubs and organizations, memberships, hobbies, and travel. At this point your goal is to come up with as much data as possible. Unnecessary information can be eliminated later in the process.

Envision this typical recruiting scenario. On Tuesday, the day after Labor Day, an employer placed an ad in a local newspaper for a sales manager's position. One-hundred-fifty resumes were received in response to the ad. Because it was an extremely busy time of the year in the company's human resources office, the employment manager decided to bring the resumes home, go through them, and select those who would be invited for interviews. The manager, whose name was Sharon, used the following process.

First she read the first line or two of each cover letter. Based on the writers' opening statements, she then made a decision about reading the resume. If she liked what she saw, she would flip over to the resume and begin to read it, looking first at the objective, next at the section on education, then at experience, and finally, at activities.

She then put the resumes into one of three stacks: Yes, No, and Maybe. Within an hour, ninety-four resumes were placed in the No stack, and twenty-six were Maybe's. Only twenty ended up in the Yes pile. Sharon did not want to interview twenty people for this position, so she then began to narrow them down from twenty to ten.

Certain criteria are generally used in the decision-making process, and Sharon used them when dividing the 150 resumes into three stacks. Employers usually make their decisions based on these criteria. On occasion there are exceptions. Referrals or a prior contact with the recruiter are two possible determinants for a Maybe or No ending up in the Yes group.

The process Sharon used for selecting interviewees is common but not universal, because each recruiter may have his or her own set of criteria for selecting or rejecting candidates. Sharon also considered cover letter and resume content and presentation.

Content criteria When you create a resume you should keep the following points in mind.

Target the employer/company/industry. Effective resumes must be targeted to the employers to whom they are mailed. Many college graduates create one all purpose resume to use in their job search. Generally this is a very ineffective self-promotion method. Employers want to see why you are specifically applying to them as well as what you are looking to do and what you have to offer. Creating a targeted resume requires that you complete both self- and world-of-work assessments. By doing this you can make sure that your background matches the position for which you are applying. Unfortunately, a commitment of both time and money is also required, as targeted resumes have to be rewritten—often. Even if you are fortunate enough to have access to a computer with a quality printer, the task is a costly one, but it is one that is worth both the cost and the effort.

Highlight your skills and accomplishments. It is imperative that your resume highlights those skills and accomplishments that meet the targeted employers' needs. Employers want to know that you already have the right type of background, the abilities, and the personality to do the job before they consider hiring you. Skills and accomplishments can be highlighted in the experience or accomplishments sections of a resume.

Be employer-oriented. When writing your objective, you should take special care to state what you can do for the employer, not what you expect an employer can do for you. Using *I* is unacceptable.

Show independence, creativity, and initiative. Most positions that require college degrees require individuals who can act independently, are creative, and show initiative. If the position you are applying for calls for these qualities, highlight them throughout your resume.

Use action verbs. When addressing your previous work and educational history, be sure to use the following action verb list. Use of these verbs creates a sense of action, making your experiences stronger.

Action Verbs List

achieved	compared	displayed	followed
acted	compiled	disproved	forecasted
adapted	completed	dissected	formulated
addressed	composed	distributed	founded
administered	computed	diverted	gathered
advertised	conceptualized	dramatized	gave
advised	conducted	drew	generated
analyzed	consolidated	drove	guided
arbitrated	constructed	dug	headed
arranged	conserved	edited	helped
ascertained	controlled	eliminated	hired
assembled	cooperated	empathized	hypothesized
assessed	coordinated	enforced	identified
assigned	copied	enlarged	illustrated
attained	counseled	enlisted	imagined
audited	created	established	implemented
authored	decided	estimated	improved
arranged	defined	evaluated	improvised
budgeted	delegated	examined	increased
built	delivered	executed	informed
calculated	demonstrated	explained	initiated
charted	designed	expanded	innovated
checked	detailed	expedited	inspected
clarified	detected	experimented	inspired
classified	determined	expressed	installed
coached	developed	extracted	instituted
consulted	devised	facilitated	instructed
collaborated	diagnosed	filed	integrated
collected	directed	financed	interpreted
communicated	discovered	fixed	interviewed

invented	persuaded	referred	stimulated
inventoried	photographed	rehabilitated	supervised
investigated	piloted	related	supplied
judged	planned	rendered	surveyed
lectured	predicted	repaired	symbolized
led	prepared	reported	synergized
learned	prescribed	represented	synthesized
listened	presented	researched	systematized
logged	presided	resolved	taught
maintained	printed	responded	team-built
managed	problem-solved	restored	tended
manipulated	processed	retrieved	tested and proved
marketed	produced	reviewed	told
mediated	programmed	revised	took instruction
memorized	projected	risked	trained
mentored	promoted	scheduled	transcribed
met	proofread	selected	translated
modeled	protected	sensed	traveled
modified	provided	separated	troubleshot
monitored	publicized	served	tutored
motivated	published	set	typed
navigated	purchased	set up	understudied
negotiated	questioned	shaped	undertook
observed	raised	shared	unified
obtained	realized	showed	united
offered	reasoned	sketched	upgraded
operated	received	sold	updated
ordered	recognized for	solved	used
organized	reconciled	sorted	weighed
originated	recommended	spoke	worked
oversaw	recorded	studied	wrote
perceived	recruited	standardized	verbalized
performed	reduced		

Use only accurate and honest information. All information that is included on your resume should be accurate and honest. You must be able to prove the facts you have stated. Employers are sometimes suspicious of individuals who build up their resumes so much that they sound too good to be true. In such cases, the individual risks ending the search process before even getting a chance for an interview.

Give numbers and percentages. Whenever possible, use numbers and percentages that will demonstrate your accomplishments. These make a good impression on the reader, as they are easy to understand and quantify your qualifications.

Show your ability to communicate. Resumes and cover letters are two documents that give you an opportunity to show how well you express yourself. They also reveal your writing style and your written communication skills. Employers pay close attention to phrasing, grammar, typos, and clarity. They often make decisions on this information alone, and, in fact, many discard resumes that contain typos. If your resume is poorly written and you are applying for a position that requires good writing skills, you will be eliminated early in the process.

Show progression academically and/or professionally. History that shows you have ability to improve and develop further as a student, professional, and individual is important to employers. If you have increased your grade point average throughout your college career, been promoted in a work situation, or been elected to an office, point it out; don't be shy.

Illustrate a sense of community. The focus of the 1990s is community commitment. Corporate America has adopted the attitude that community is important, and companies want their employees to participate in community affairs, because it is good for the company. Be sure and list your contributions to your community, college, workplace, or hometown. Employers are impressed with a proven history of giving, for they believe that history will repeat itself and that when you are an employee, you will continue this pattern on behalf of the company.

Minimize personal data. Personal information should only be included in your resume if it is required for the position for which you are applying, and very few positions require this information. Religious and political affiliations, height, weight, marital status, birth dates, and social security numbers are personal and need not be on any resume. Because this type of information can be used in a discriminatory manner, it is unlawful for employers to ask personal questions. Do not give them this information voluntarily.

Presentation criteria

In considering resume presentation, keep these points in mind.

Use a simple, clear approach. The test for a simple, clear resume is whether it can be skimmed in thirty seconds or less. It should give the reader an accurate sense of who you are and clearly state what you have to offer, without creating doubts or leaving a negative impression.

Use a one-page resume. New college graduates generally do not require a two- or three-page resume; most don't have the experience or background to warrant it. There are some new graduates, however, especially those who have received their degrees through a continuing education program, who do have years of experience to offer. If possible, they, too, should use a one-page format for their resumes.

Ask yourself the question, "Do I want to get an interview?" If you do, narrow your resume down to only the information that is pertinent to the position under consideration. Although there are exceptions, it is generally best to use a layout that requires one page.

Use professional printing. A laser printer or, at the very least, a top-line typewriter will create the professional look you want to project. You have to present yourself on paper as someone as good as or better than everybody else who is applying for the position. If you don't have access to a computer system with a good printer, allowing you to make changes easily, use two or three different resumes, differentiated by objective statements. These can be professionally printed while remaining cost-effective.

Select proper paper and color. The rule of thumb here is to use a bond weight resume paper that is available at any good print shop. Color should reflect the industry to which you will be applying. If you are seeking a position in the banking industry (typically conservative), use a conservative color: off-white, light gray, or beige. On the other hand, the advertising or retail industries (fairly liberal) are more accepting of softer pastels: blues, light green, or even peach. Avoid the fate of the "orchid stationery" user by studying the industry culture before making your purchase.

Use a consistent format. Your resume layout will affect the reader's ability to pull out information of importance. Consistency throughout is the rule. If you put dates in the left column in one section, then do it that way throughout. All resumes should have a one-inch margin around the perimeter.

Proofread and pay attention to detail. After all the hard work that you put into your resume, it is important to proofread it very carefully, both for typographical errors and minor inconsistencies. Nothing seems to upset a potential employer more than a typo. It is a good idea to have someone who has never seen your resume proofread it for you. You have been so close to it that you may not be able to identify typos or mistakes. One suggestion for catching typos is to read the resume backwards word by word.

Resume components

The heading of your resume should include your full name, address, and phone number. Many college seniors may want to use both their current college and permanent addresses. It is imperative that you include at least one daytime phone number. Nothing frustrates an employer more than not being able to reach an applicant to set up an interview. Even when you state in your cover letter that you will make a follow-up call, the employer may try to call you first. Include a phone number in the heading.

Heading Information Exercise:

Name _____

Address #1 _____

City, State, Zip Code _____

Phone Number _____

Address #2 _____

City, State, Zip Code _____

Phone Number _____

The objective is difficult to state, yet it is one of the most important parts of a resume because it sets the tone for the rest of the document. Since it is the first thing the reader sees, it is important that your objective attracts attention.

An objective should state the type of position you are seeking and the industry of interest to you. For example: *A social worker position in the state mental health care system.*

Some experts suggest inclusion of a brief statement about your willingness to travel or relocate, your skills, or your desire for a position of responsibility along with your objective. Every objective should be brief and specific, realistic, and individually tailored to the job for which you are applying. An objective that indicates you have given some thought to your career goals will impress a prospective employer.

Is it absolutely necessary to include an objective in your resume? Some say it is. Others disagree. Realize that resumes are individual marketing tools. On some occasions it may be more appropriate not to include an objective, especially if you cannot afford the high cost of typing individual resumes or if you have varied interests that are hard to represent in one statement. In eliminating an objective, you are taking a risk with employers who want to see one on a prospect's resume.

Your objective, when used, is the starting point from which the reader makes his or her decision to interview or not to interview. If your objective statement is not related to the position for which you are applying, your resume will probably end up in the No stack.

Remember, too, everything that follows the objective must support your candidacy for the position. If you choose not to include an objective, then very clearly state the position you are seeking in the first paragraph of your cover letter.

Suggested objective headings include Professional Objective, Career Objective, Employment Objective, Job Objective, or Goal. Select whichever one you believe fits your special situation or needs.

Objective Exercise:

OBJECTIVE: _____

_____

OBJECTIVE: _____

_____

Education. For most new college graduates, education should be placed next on the resume. It is in this prominent position because it is what you are selling to employers. The section on education includes information about the college or university from which you graduated; your degree program, including majors and minors; location of the college or university; and the month and year that you received your degree. If you have not graduated at the time you are putting together a resume, it is perfectly acceptable to state that you anticipate a degree or are a degree candidate. Give the date you expect to receive your degree so that employers will know you will have it by the time you are available for employment.

If you have more than one degree, place the most recent one first. Employers are sometimes more interested in seeing what degree you hold than they are in the institution from which it was received. It is up to you to decide where to place education information and what areas to highlight. As said above, it is important for new graduates to position the education section at the beginning of the resume. After a few years of good professional experience, you need not place it up front.

Other pertinent information that can fall under the education section includes grade point average, honors and awards, course work, expenses you contributed to your college education, foreign language, and computer language ability.

There is much debate as to the importance of the GPA and its relationship to performance on the job. Many employers want to see it when making decisions about employment. Should you, then, include it in your resume? In making your decision, use the following guidelines: If applying for a technical position, such as accounting or engineering, include it if it is over a 3.3 on a scale of 4.0. If you are applying for a nontechnical position, such as one in sales, include a GPA only if it is a 3.0 or over. If your GPA should fall below these baselines, it does not mean that you will not be interviewed, but it is best not to raise any doubt about your ability by putting a 2.2 GPA on your resume. Use your discretion. Employers will always ask, if a GPA is an important factor in their decision-making process. Also, if you have great depth of experience or a current relationship with the employer in question, your GPA will carry less weight because these other factors will have an impact on the decision to interview you.

Honors and awards must be included on your resume. If you have a list of honors and awards create a separate section for them, either in the education section or in a later section. Be sure to place all honors related to education in one section. Examples of educational awards include graduating cum laude, being on the dean's list, and being listed in *Who's Who*.

A related courses section is generally used for one of two reasons: to promote your theoretical knowledge of a subject or to fill the gap on an otherwise empty resume. Don't bother listing this information for any other reason. It takes up space that could be used for more important facts.

It is certainly acceptable to include a statement that tells an employer the percentage of your college expenses that you yourself earned. Such a statement shows responsibility, motivation, and energy. Include dollars earned through scholarships, full- or part-time work. This statement is more impressive if you contributed 50 percent or more of your educational expenses. Many continuing education graduates earn 100 percent of their expenses.

If you have foreign language ability or skills related to computer use, in either hardware, software, or language, include them on your resume. Whether they belong in the education section or deserve their own separate area depends upon how strong these abilities are and their relationship to the position for which you are applying.

Suggested education headings include Education, Educational Background, Educational Credentials, Academic Training, Higher Education. Choose whichever you feel suits you best.

Education Information Exercise:

Degree #1: _____

College: _____

Address: _____

City, State: _____

GPA: _____

Degree #2: _____

College: _____

Address: _____

City, State: _____

GPA: _____

Honors/Awards: _____

Course Work: _____

_____

Expenses Statement: _____

Languages/Computer Skills: _____

_____

The experience section is probably the lengthiest and most difficult to write. In preparing to write this section, you must list all of the paying and nonpaying work experiences, including internships and/or co-op ed experiences that you have had up to this point in your life. Don't think about any of the job specifics, just write the name of the company, and, if you had one, your title. If you didn't have a title, give yourself one. If you completed the experience exercise in the interest section, you may find it helpful to refer back to it.

Position #1 _____ Company: _____

Position #2 _____ Company: _____

Position #3 _____ Company: _____

Position #4 _____ Company: _____

Position #5 _____ Company: _____

Position #6 _____ Company: _____

Now, take a separate piece of paper and jot down all of the duties you had in each position. Try and come up with as much as data as possible. Ask yourself:

- What did I accomplish?
- How would I describe a typical day on the job to someone unfamiliar with it?
- What did I create or develop on the job?
- What did I learn most in the position?

It is important to give yourself credit for everything you did. Many college graduates forget about the value of being a camp counselor, a summer construction worker, or a waitperson.

Next, review and analyze all of the data that you have collected for each of the positions and, using resume language, create statements that accurately describe your skills and abilities, strengths, and positions of responsibility. Be sure each job demonstrates progress. Come up with short, easy-to-read phrases, using the action verb list provided on page 77. Write to the interest of the prospective employer. The statements describing each position can be either bulleted or written in a paragraph format. Just be sure they are relevant to the employer and the position you are seeking.

Employment Experience Exercise:

Title: _____

Employer: _____

Dates of Employment: _____

Description: _____

_____

_____

_____

Title: _____

Employer: _____

Dates of Employment: _____

Description: _____

_____

_____

_____

Title: _____

Employer: _____

Dates of Employment: _____

Description: _____

_____

_____

_____

In their first attempt at resume writing, most people write either too little or too much. The key to success is to use only relevant data that supports your objective and will be of interest to the reader. This is the place to use numbers and percentages, as they are to the point and easy to follow. Increasing sales by 50 percent means a lot to a sales manager. Use it to reinforce your ability.

The following are examples of properly written text that describe positions held while in college.

- Conducted library research for the University of California project on U.S. voting statistics. Compiled census data for all U.S. congressional districts from 1950 to the present.

- Developed a credit and collection system that reduced receivables from sixty-five to forty-five days. This added $300,000 to the cash flow and reduced interest expenses by $35,000 annually.

- Assisted students with learning difficulties in various courses, including physics, calculus, statistics, accounting, and economics. Taught students study and note-taking techniques in preparation for exams.

- Coordinated and organized support activities for a variety of community-based human service and non-profit organizations.

As mentioned, many students do not list jobs as waitpersons or secretaries. These jobs have great value, as they show that you have experienced teamwork and responsibility. Don't leave them out unless you can't get all the information into your one-page format. Don't say that you were only a waitress or waiter. Employers repeatedly say that such positions are important in developing a work ethic, understanding the importance of customer service, and learning to deal with repetition. Spend enough time developing this segment of your resume; it is worth it. It also prepares you to answer tough interview questions.

In writing the experience section of your resume, be sure it answers the questions, "How will this person meet my needs?" or "Does he or she have the ability to contribute from day one?" Let employers know what you have to offer!!

Suggested experience headings include Related Experience, Professional Experience, Work Experience, Other Employment, Qualifications, Professional Involvement. Choose the one that best fits your situation.

One question often raised is, "What should I do if my most-related experience is not my most recent experience?" The answer to this is to use two sections to highlight your experience: the first one entitled Related Experience and the second, Other Experience. This way you can highlight the related experience without leaving gaps on your resume.

Memberships. If you have been active in professional associations or clubs, then you may want to utilize a membership section. Affiliation and teambuilding are important to employers. Your past participation signifies your interest in a particular field as well as your desire to interact professionally with members of industry.

Suggested membership headings include Professional Affiliations, Professional Associations, Conferences.

Membership Exercise:

Memberships: _____ Dates: _____
_____ Dates: _____

Honors. This section highlights your success at school or in the workplace. History does repeat itself, and employers are looking for individuals with a proven history. If you are above average, say so!

Honors Exercise:

_____

_____

Activities. This section should include all activities or involvement on campus and in the community. It could include memberships, if not in a separate section, affiliations, or participation in extracurricular programs. This is a "catch-all" section that tells an employer you have been active, and have not just stayed in your room studying or spent your college days at all-night parties. Employers like active, well-rounded people.

Activities Exercise:

Activities: _____

_____

_____

Interests. This is usually the weakest section in a resume, and for that reason, you may not use it. As with personal information, its time has past. Your interests should stand out on your resume through your activities and involvement. It's one thing to say you like to do something and another to actually do it.

References. This area of the resume has come under debate in recent years. If you have something better to put in its place then by all means do so. Employers are going to ask for references if they are interested in you, whether you state it on your resume or not. Unless requested, don't submit or list references as part of your resume. If you are required to submit references with your resume, write them on a separate piece of paper. College seniors should check with their institutions' career offices for their policy on placement files and references. Using a statement such as "References furnished upon request" is generally sufficient.

Resume formats

Once you have developed the information for each resume section, you are ready to create the total promotional tool. You will need to decide what resume format will best market your talents and abilities. There are two styles that you can use: chronological or functional.

The chronological resume is best suited for traditional college graduates in the traditional age group (21–24). It is the format most familiar to employers. It is straightforward, highlights educational and work experience in chronological order (most recent first), and emphasizes career growth. It also highlights previous employment, job titles, and dates of employment and includes a succinct description of the activities performed in each position. It emphasizes duties and achievements and stresses experience. If your work history has been less than stable, don't use this format; it will only make it more apparent. Samples of chronological resumes can be found on pages 92–94.

JODI L. TULL

Permanent Address
28 Surrey Lane
Livingston, NJ 07039
201-555-1492

College Address
2500 North River Road
Manchester, NH 03104
603-555-2076

EDUCATION NEW HAMPSHIRE COLLEGE, MANCHESTER, NEW HAMPSHIRE
Bachelor of Science Degree in Marketing, May 1992

TEL AVIV UNIVERSITY, TEL AVIV, ISRAEL
Intensive Hebrew Language course, Summer 1990

UNIVERSITY OF ARIZONA, TUCSON, ARIZONA
Visiting student. Fall 1991

AWARDS WHO'S WHO AMONG STUDENTS IN AMERICAN COLLEGES AND UNIVERSITIES, 1991

EXPERIENCE

1991 (Fall) ETCETRA, TUCSON, ARIZONA
SALES ASSOCIATE (SPECIALTY RETAIL OPERATION)
- **Sold** women's accessories
- **Achieved** recognition as top salesperson for the fall period
- **Performed** all retail duties

1991 (Summer) KENNEDY WILSON, INC., WEST ORANGE, NEW JERSEY
CUSTOMER RELATIONS REPRESENTATIVE (AUCTION CO.)
- **Registered, hosted,** and **provided** information on condominium sales to potential buyers.

1991 (Summer) AMERICAN TRAILS WEST, GREAT NECK, NEW YORK
COUNSELOR (SUMMER TRAVELING CAMP)
- **Supervised** seven week East Coast travel program for 40 teenagers
- **Provided** total care and safety of participants including medical, social, educational, and travel needs

1990 (Fall) SAKS FIFTH AVENUE, NEW YORK, NEW YORK
MANAGEMENT COOPERATIVE EDUCATION EXPERIENCE
- **Promoted** from Assistant Manager in Women's Activewear Department to Gift Certificate Operation Department Manager six weeks into co-op semester
- **Established** and managed $2 million department during Christmas season
- **Supervised, scheduled** and **trained** 13 sales staff
- **Worked** closely with General Managers and V.P.

1988–1990 NHC ADMISSIONS OFFICE, MANCHESTER, NEW HAMPSHIRE
TOUR GUIDE/RECRUITING COORDINATOR
- **Guided** prospective students through campus and answered all questions pertaining to the college
- **Provided** information about the college and called students to schedule campus visits

ACTIVITIES NEW HAMPSHIRE COLLEGE

Varsity Tennis Team
Student Government Association Representative
Orientation Leader
Marketing Academy Representative
International Big Sister Representative
New England Association of Campus Activities
Earth Day 1990 Coordinating Committee

REFERENCES Furnished upon request

David Kidwell
62 Burbank Boulevard
Hollywood, Florida
(818) 555-0001

OBJECTIVE A management trainee position in the banking/investment industry

EDUCATION Bachelor of Science Degree, June 1991
Florida University
Major: Economics/Finance

Selected Courses related to objective:
- Corporate Finance
- Money & Banking
- Managerial Economics
- Systems Analysis
- Introduction to Investments
- Financial Policy & Decision Making
- Micro & Macroeconomics
- Business Ethics

COMPUTER SKILLS BASIC Programming, Lotus 1–2–3, Multimate 3.3, WordPerfect 5.0, and PFS First Choice

HONORS AND ACTIVITIES
- Dean's List (3 semesters)
- President/Founder Economics & Finance Association
- Learning Center Tutor (Math, Finance, and Computers)
- Yearbook Committee
- Kappa Delta Phi National Fraternity:
  - Purchasing Agent (ordered products, worked with accountant)
  - Philanthropy Committee Worker (Volunteer worker for Red Cross, Salvation Army, New Horizons Soup Kitchen)

EXPERIENCE **Landscaper/Painter:** Summer 1990
The Kidwell Company, Hollywood, Fla.
Pruned, painted homes, did interior home maintenance

Parts Department Manager: Summer 1989
Turf Products Corporation (TPC), Miami, Fla.
Stocked inventory, received customer orders, checked quality of products sent to customers

General Laborer: Summer 1988
Ergee International, Miami, Fla.
Gathered products and shipped orders to customers

Private First Class: November 1986 to September 1987
Florida Army National Guard, HQ2-181, Gainesville, Fla.
Computer input operator of military operating procedures. Prepared pay statements. Honorably Discharged.

Clerk: Spring 1986 to Fall 1987
Consumer Value Stores (CVS), Gainesville, Fla.
Interacted with customers, worked registers, organized stock, advised setup locations for products and promotional sales.

REFERENCES AVAILABLE UPON REQUEST

CHRONOLOGICAL

VIRGINIA F. TESSEY

Permanent Address
22 Summer Street
Waterbury, ME 04904
(207) 555-6820

College Address
Baystate College
16 North Street, Box 6931
Baltimore, MD 03267

OBJECTIVE   A position in, or leading to, management in the hospitality industry.

EDUCATION   State College, Baltimore, MD
Bachelor of Science degree in Hotel Management, May 1991
Strong concentration in Marketing

Lansdowne College, London, England, Spring 1990

HONORS
- Dean's list 7 semesters (GPA 3.4/4.0)
- Alumni Academic Scholarship (4 years)
- Admissions Scholarship (4 years)
- Delta Mu Delta National Honor Society
- Who's Who Among Students in American Universities and Colleges, 1990–1991

ACTIVITIES
- **Ambassador of State College**. One of seven students chosen by President of Baystate to represent the college at community functions.
- **Special Events Committee**. Chairperson. Organize and plan two of the largest weekends on campus.
- **Student Government Association**. Junior class chair; executive assistant on executive board.
- **S.H.A.R.P.** Students Helping Admissions Recruiting Program, Secretary.
- **Yearbook Staff**
- **Intramural Sports**

EXPERIENCE   **Tour Guide/Interviewer/Telemarketer**
State College Admissions Office, 1988–Present
Lead prospective students and their parents throughout campus, interview students and speak at other admissions functions. Call prospective students to schedule campus visits and provide information about the college.

Bartender and Waitress, Classics Restaurant
Waterville, ME, May–Sept. 1990
Train new employees for positions and assist management with daily operations.

Internship, Wychmere Harbor Hotel
Harwichport, MA, May–Sept. 1989
Train at front desk and sales. Successful completion of all tasks for credit.

REFERENCES AVAILABLE UPON REQUEST

For older graduates or career changers, the chronological style resume may highlight gaps. If you have gaps in your employment history, you may find it more advantageous to use a functional resume.

The functional resume is not as familiar to employers as the chronological, but for some job seekers it may be the best format to use, as it focuses on your functional or transferable skills. By way of illustration, consider Mary whose prior work experience includes a work-study position in her university athletic facility, waitressing in a restaurant, a sales position in a retail fashion store, and a summer job with a local parks and recreation department. This is good experience, but not directly related to her objective of becoming a management trainee in a bank.

There are, however, common threads to her various positions that she can bring to the attention of her potential employer. Each position she held required leadership skills, the ability to manage time, and an element of planning. All of these skills are required of a management trainee in the banking industry. Mary therefore chose to use the functional style resume to highlight her three skills areas. The purpose of using this style is to focus on skills, not titles, company, or dates of employment. Although that information is also included in a functional resume, it is not the focal point. A functional resume allows considerable flexibility, while playing on strong areas of ability.

Examples of skills that can be highlighted in a functional resume are leadership, public speaking, sales, training, organizational, research, counseling, and public relations. This style works well for college graduates who are currently looking to make career changes or for those who want to emphasize skills gained through employment, especially when they have little experience in a chosen career field. One drawback of the functional resume style is that some employers are not familiar with it.

Whatever style resume you choose to use, it is important that you ask yourself the following questions before finalizing your format.

- Are you comfortable with your resume?
- Have you marketed your skills, abilities, experience, and education effectively?
- Will you be able to support your resume with examples in an interview?

If you are able to answer "yes" to all three of these questions, then march forward with confidence, knowing that your resume will be a successful component of your strategic self-marketing plan.

FUNCTIONAL

SALLY SMITH
99 Circus Lane
Java, NY 11560
(509) 767-0001

EDUCATION: **Bachelor of Arts, Business and Economics,** May 1991
Mount Anselm College, Manchester, VT
Self-financed 60% of college education expenses

EXPERIENCE:

Leadership and Organization:
- Served as editor of International Affairs section of college newspaper including identification and assignment of leads to staff.
- Developed public relations, managerial and delegatory skills as chief organizer of and speaker at the Annual College Academic Investiture Ceremony.
- Creatively planned children's activities for 200 participants at Mt. Sunapee Fair fund-raiser.
- Founded campus Political Awareness Club and developed proposals for funding and recruiting members.
- Contributed to the success of Annual College Holiday Festival for 150 needy area children as committee member and participant.
- Effectively coordinated function room and press corner preparation prior to national presidential campaign; developed relationships with aides and supervised a staff of 10 people.

Communications:
- Contributed articles to two college newspapers.
- Conducted constructive discussions in groups such as the Political Awareness Club.
- Counseled troubled women in crisis through an outreach agency.
- Represented student interests through Student Government involvement.

Computer Literacy:
- Competent on the IBM System 36, the NCR proof machine, and the Macintosh Plus System. Used numerous business software packages including Accounting and Operations management "simplex Method" on a VAX. Have innovatively designed spreadsheets and graphics on Lotus 1–2–3 software. Trained co-workers on same.

WORK HISTORY: **Computer Operator,** Hillsboro Bank and Trust
Milford, Vt. (Full & Part time, June 1988–February 1991)
Data Processor & Executive Office Assistant,
Norel Temporary Services, Winston, NY
(Full & Part time, May 1987–May 1988)
Cashier, Alexander's Supermarket, Austin, NY (July 1986–August 1988)

FUNCTIONAL

Eddie Andrews
14 Chapel Street, Apartment 24
Newmarket, California 93857
(608) 658-1299

OBJECTIVE: An entry level management position in the financial services industry.

MANAGEMENT:
- Handled personnel duties for a staff of 8 to 17.
- Managed a $200,000 department inventory.

TRAINING:
- Trained five members of the current Yankee Bargain Stores' management team.
- Contributed half of all Yankee Bargain Stores written procedures.

COMMUNICATION:
- Developed the cash control system and trained all Yankee Bargain Store managers in its use.
- Tutored college Freshmen and Sophomores in finite math.

PLANNING:
- Created a computer database to be used for sales projections.
- Designed and reset store's floor layout.
- Set up one new store.
- Established the computer system for Yankee Bargain Stores.

EMPLOYMENT:
1985–1989   *Yankee Bargain Stores:*
- Store Manager, Oakland, CA
- Assistant Manager, Sacramento, CA
- Head Cashier, Oakland, CA

1988   *Harold's Discount Depot*, Newmarket, CA
- Administrative Assistant to Store Manager

1984   *Burke College*, Oakland, CA
- Math Tutor/Teaching Assistant

EDUCATION:
- Burke College, Oakland, CA, B.S. 1987
  Major: Economics/Finance
  Minor: Computer Information Systems

***Some final resume
comments***

Remember that resumes are screening tools. There may be times when one won't be needed for an interview; however, employers usually do like one for screening purposes. The important thing to remember about your resume is that it must be just as good as, if not better (in both content and presentation), than the others that end up in the Yes stack. Take enough time and energy to prepare the best resume that you can. Make it one that represents you at your best. Employers do make decisions based upon this one piece of paper. Right or wrong, it's reality!

Of course, there will always be exceptions to the guidelines that have been set forth here. All individuals have different circumstances in their lives. When you put your resume together, think about it from an employer's perspective and remember the scenario where Sharon had to make some tough choices based upon one piece of paper. You will not get selected every time you send out a resume, but there are things that you can do to increase your odds. First, create a document that represents you, and second, send it for appropriate positions only. Many people send resumes en masse. This is almost always a waste of energy, time, and money.

You might want to keep these factors in mind:

1. If you were to show your resume to a hundred people, each one would give you a hundred different suggestions on how to improve it. Many of them would be worthy; some would not.

2. Ultimately, it is you and only you who makes the decision about the resume that best represents you.

3. You will not always be able to predict what an employer will like in a resume; following the suggestions in this section can improve your odds of getting an interview.

4. There are many ways to write a resume. Be sure that yours represents "the best" you to an employer.

5. A resume and cover letter, even if perfectly done, will not always guarantee an interview since any advertised position may generate a resume response of between 50 and 250-plus resumes. Sometimes it is a game of chance.

The Effective Cover Letter

While your resume should receive great attention and importance in your self-promotion campaign, your cover letter is equally important when marketing yourself to employers. The cover letter precedes your resume. It introduces you to potential employers and acts as another self-promotional tool. If properly written, it will receive a favorable response from employers, and they will invite you to interview for a position. Because an employer may read only part or none of your cover letter before glancing at your resume, be sure that your opening paragraph is an "attention getter."

Prior to writing a resume, you completed a self-assessment. While doing this you examined your work and life values, skills, and areas of interest. The information gained while doing the self-assessment exercise portion of your self-marketing plan can be very helpful when applying for specific positions and in writing cover letters.

A good cover letter should tell employers how you can meet their needs. It should not be a carbon copy of your resume. Your ability to write such a letter is a major factor in attainment of your employment goal. Cover letters should give employers reasons to want to meet and interview you, and they should add spice to the factual information in your resume.

The contents of a cover letter tell employers your reasons for writing and what you have to offer. Your closing should indicate what you would like to have happen after your letter has been read. All cover letters should be strong in terms of content, style, and presentation.

Content criteria

The introduction—state why you are writing. There are many different reasons why you may be sending a cover letter and resume to an employer. The position may be advertised (solicited), you may be responding to an article or publication in which the company was listed or mentioned (unsolicited), or you may be writing as a result of a referral. Here are a few examples.

- Solicited cover letter—"I read about your opening for a Marketing Coordinator in the May 22, 1992, issue of the *Jobline.*"

- Unsolicited cover letter—"In reading the 1992 CPC Annual, I noted your company was interested in English majors for positions in your editing department."

- Referral cover letter—"Glen Morton, Human Resource Director at MNO Corporation, has informed me that you are looking to fill a sales manager's position."

Your introduction should get and keep the attention of the reader. If it doesn't, the resume you spent so much time preparing may never even get the usual glance.

Middle paragraph(s)—tell what you have to offer. In this section, which generally covers a second and possibly a third paragraph, you need to show an employer how your skills and experience can meet their needs. To isolate their needs, you will have to research the organization. Do not duplicate your resume in this section; rather, enhance your resume content and reveal your personality through your writing style. Be sure to stress previous achievements that parallel an employer's needs and show that you are qualified to fill the position. Accentuate the positive! Examples:

- "My experience as a teacher's aide has heightened my desire to pursue a career in elementary education."
- "As a member of the Phi Kappa Delta Fraternity I strengthened my sales skills when I was chair of a fund-raising campaign. Funds raised surpassed previous years' goals by 40 percent."
- "Waitressing taught me to work well under pressure and to respond appropriately to people's varying needs."

The closing—end with strength. In the final paragraph of your cover letter, you should take control over the expected outcome. Be assertive; let the reader know that you will follow up with a phone call, if this is possible. State when you will call and what you would like to have happen at that time. For example, "My enclosed resume outlines my work history and accomplishments. I will contact you in ten days to see if a time can be set when we can meet to discuss the opportunities at MNO Corporation."

Writing style criteria   The second major element of a cover letter is writing style. The ever-essential communication skills that all employers seek from those who hold college degrees must be demonstrated in a cover letter. Writing style refers to proper grammar, creativity, and the ability to express your thoughts in a clear, concise, direct manner.

Presentation criteria

The way a cover letter is presented is of extreme importance. Neatness, print type, paper choice, and formatting must be taken into consideration when preparing this self-promotion piece. Also, check and double-check for typographical errors. They are never acceptable.

After having spent considerable time and money on resume preparation, you need to pay attention to the appearance of your cover letter. If possible, use the same paper that you used for your resume. There are many correct ways to format a cover letter, but whichever format you choose, always make sure you line up margins and balance the body of the letter properly on the paper. For many it is not feasible to have each cover letter individually typed by a professional. If you have to use a printer that does not match your resume type, at least use the same paper.

Your resume and cover letter can be two extremely valuable self-promotion tools. If well done, they can open many interview doors. If poorly done, the doors may remain closed, and you will not have an opportunity to display your well-prepared and packaged self-product in person.

Interviewing

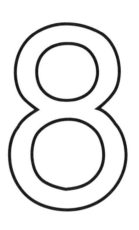

The third major tool in your self-promotion package is the interview. You will only reach this important step in the job search with proper preparation, for the recruiting, selecting, and training process is becoming so expensive for employers, with the cost of the average hire ranging from $3,000–$4,000, that those hiring college graduates are very selective and are going to fewer, very carefully chosen campuses each year. Instead of visits, they are using computerized data bases such as kiNexus[1] and Connexion[2] and are

[1]A product of Information Kinetics, Inc., of Chicago, Illinois, kiNexus links college graduates with employers through a national data base. It is available at select college campuses or by calling 312–335–0787.

[2]Connexion is Peterson's new service that links people in transition to employers and graduate schools across the country. It is available on college campuses or by writing directly to: Peterson's Connexion, PO Box 2123, Princeton, NJ 08543.

participating in job fairs in major cities where prescreened graduates and alumni from different colleges and universities are in attendance. Cost-effectiveness will continue to be a high priority with employers throughout the decade.

If you have completed a self-assessment and have developed a good sense of the areas in the world of work that interest you, you are well on your way to being prepared for any job interview and personal contact with an employer. If you haven't already completed the self-assessment in section 2 go back and do the exercises now.

All contact that you have with an employer during the job-search process, either at a job fair, over the telephone, or at an information session on campus, offers you an opportunity to sell yourself. If you are ill prepared, personal contact can also be the rope by which you hang yourself. Human resource representatives, managers, and others in the hiring process are usually well trained to screen out those candidates who are not prepared to interview.

Here are some reasons why candidates are not chosen.

- Poor grooming
- Lack of vitality or enthusiasm
- Aggressive, cynical, or superior behavior
- Poor verbal skills
- No expression of career goals
- Obvious lack of self-confidence
- Failure to participate in college or community activities
- Concentration on pay only
- Poor academic record
- Evasiveness
- Lack of tact, maturity, and courtesy
- Condemnation of past employers
- Obvious dislike for schoolwork
- Failure to look interviewer in the eye
- Limp handshake
- Lack of knowledge about career field
- No interest in the employer
- Visable laziness

- Intolerance of others
- Inability to take criticism
- Late arrival without good reason
- Lack of knowledge about the employer

The interview process must be taken seriously if you want to receive a job offer, but you don't have to lose sleep, become ill, or have panic attacks. All applicants experience anxiety as they begin the process. Interviewing does not come naturally; it is a learned skill that you can develop through practice. Mock interviews are one method of learning what an interview will be like. Mock interviewing with a career professional, human resource representative, family member, or friend will enable you to pull your thoughts together prior to an interview with an employer. Video-taped mock interviews are even more helpful because they allow you to watch your performance objectively and they help you become aware of your body language.

Most college graduates can benefit from a mock interview prior to their first professional one. Consider Patty, a graduate from New Hampshire College, scheduled to interview with a financial services organization at a New Jersey recruiting fair. She was, to say the least, a nervous wreck. She had never had an interview before and she realized that her competitors were graduates from some very well known colleges in the New Jersey area. Frozen with fear, she sat and waited for her turn. To her credit, she did complete the interview and survived to talk about it. She also learned a very valuable lesson. PRACTICE, PRACTICE, PRACTICE! If she had participated in the mock interview programs offered by the college's career development center she could have alleviated some of her anxiety prior to the interview and helped herself conquer the biggest fear of all, fear of the unknown.

If you think of an interview as a two-way conversation you will not be overwhelmed. Granted, the employer may choose not to offer you the position even if you are relaxed, but you certainly won't do well at all if you are frightened. Being overly nervous will not get you a job. Put things into perspective and try to display an upbeat attitude. It will take you much further than fear due to lack of preparation.

The interview is the time when you can finally make a presentation of your skills and personality. For the prospective employer it is a chance to meet you, assess your qualifications, your communications skills, and motivations. During the interview employers are asking themselves, "Is this the best person suited for the job?" At the same time, you are asking yourself, "Is this the company where I want to work?"

Employers are human! Remember that. They do not expect you to be perfect. On the contrary, they are looking for someone with personality and who is at ease with himself or herself and with life in general. If you doubt your skills in this area, the key word is, PRACTICE! Assistance from an experienced professional who can help you learn more about interviewing will also help you develop self-confidence.

Going into the interview you have three goals:

1. To demonstrate clearly that you are the person for the position.

2. To let the interviewer know all about your relevant work history. (If they don't ask, tell them.)

3. To gather enough information about the job, company, and industry to make an educated decision.

There are many reasons why candidates are chosen by an employer. They include:

1. Good communications skills

2. Initiative, energy, and enthusiasm

3. Clear motivation to do well in the position

4. Assertiveness

5. Ability to market oneself

6. Goal orientation

7. Intelligence and analytical ability

8. Both team and leadership qualities

9. Problem-solving and decision-making abilities

10. Technical skills and related work experience

11. Creativity and flexibility

12. Maturity

13. Good work habits

These are the major reasons an employer makes the decision to continue through the interview process and eventually make an offer. Show that you meet these criteria during every interview.

Preparing for the Interview

In preparing for the interview, you need to research the company and, if possible, the interviewer.

Researching a company includes knowing the industry in general as well as the particular company. It means knowing the number of employees in the company and knowing how many branch offices or plants there are and their locations. Know if there is a parent company or subsidiaries. Investigate the company's current and recent financial standing and find out if it has recent or future merger or acquisition plans. You also want to find out about the products or services made or sold, why people like or don't like the company, who the competition is, and where the company stands compared to its competition. Finally, get a sense of the salary range for the position being offered. Most basic information is easily available from annual reports and company public relations materials. These will also help you gain a better understanding of the company culture and management style. But don't stop there. Anyone can get these reports. Because you want to set yourself apart from your competition in the interview process, in addition to reading, speak with people who work in the organization and with customers. Journal articles about the industry are also good sources of information.

The best and quickest way of researching a position of interest is to ask for a written job description so as to learn the basic duties, responsibilities, and skills required to do well in the job.

Know who will be interviewing you, what his or her position is in the company. Will it be a human resource representative or a first-line manager? There is a difference between the interviewing styles of the two. Human resource professionals tend to hold more of a screening interview, whereas first-line managers ask more technical questions that relate to the position.

Know yourself

You can prepare for future interviews by practicing your answers to the commonly asked interview questions listed below. You may not be asked questions that are worded exactly as the ones on this list, but studying them will help you to answer any questions that an employer may ask you during the interview.

Questions that you may be asked during an interview

1. What are your short-term and long-term professional goals?

2. What do you really want to do in life?

3. What are your long-range career objectives?

4. How do you plan to achieve your career goals?

5. What are the most important rewards you expect during your career years?

6. What do you want or expect to be earning in five years?

7. Why did you choose the career path for which you are preparing?

8. What is more important for you: the money or the job?

9. What do you consider to be your greatest strengths and weaknesses?

10. How would you describe yourself?

11. What do you think a friend or professor who knows you would say about you?

12. What motivates you to put forth your greatest efforts?

13. How has your college experience prepared you for a career in _____?

14. Why should I hire you?

15. What qualifications do you have that make you think you will be successful in _____?

16. How do you determine or evaluate success?

17. What do you think it takes to be successful in a company like ours?

18. What qualities should a successful manager possess?

19. Describe the relationship that should exist between a manager and those reporting to him or her.

20. What three accomplishments have given you the most satisfaction?

21. Describe your most rewarding college experience?

22. Why did you select your college or university?

23. What led you to choose _____ as your field of study?

24. What college subjects did you like the best? The least? Why?

25. If you could do so, would you plan your academic study differently?

26. Do you have plans to continue your education?

27. Do you think that your grade point average is a good indication of your academic achievement?

28. What have you learned from participation in extracurriculur activities?

29. In what kind of work environment are you most comfortable?

30. How do you work under pressure?

31. In what co-op ed/internship or part-time experience have you been most interested?

32. How would you describe the ideal job for you following graduation?

33. Why did you decide to seek a position with this company?

34. What two or three things are most important to you in your job?

35. Are you seeking employment in a company of a certain size?

36. What criteria are you using to evaluate the company for which you hope to work?

37. Do you have a geographical preference?

38. Will you relocate? Does relocation bother you?

39. Are you willing to travel?

40. Are you willing to spend nine months as a trainee?

41. What were your favorite classes in college?

42. What do you think a fair salary would be?

43. What do you know about our company's products or services?

44. Describe your least favorite boss or teacher.

45. Describe your last job.

46. What skills do you have?

47. What have you learned from your mistakes?

48. Why do you want to change careers?

49. Why did you leave your present position?

50. What related experience and/or skills do you bring to this industry?

Knock Em Dead, published by Bob Adams, Inc., is a very helpful resource on interviewing that provides insight into why employers ask the questions they do. It also provides information that will help you formulate answers that both highlight your strengths and address the employers' concerns.

The Interview Itself Arrive at the site fifteen minutes earlier than you are scheduled to interview. If you are traveling long distances or are unaware of the area, give yourself more time, possibly spending the night at a local hotel or with family or friends in the area.

When you arrive, take a few minutes to pull yourself together, visit the restroom, and make sure that you look your very best. Sit in the lobby or reception area and notice all that is happening around you. Notice the people who are walking around and the interaction that occurs. Read any literature that is available and strike up a conversation with others in the area. Be careful what you say; you never know who you are speaking with or what relationship the person has to your future boss—or if the person is your future boss. When interacting with support staff make the most positive impression you can; it may help out in the long run.

Introduction As previously stated, the employer is human and may also experience some anxiety during the interview. The interviewer is certainly aware of your nervousness, as he or she at one time in the past has been on your side of the table. Interviewers want to put you at ease. The last thing they want is to spend thirty or so minutes with a stressed-out interviewee.

At the opening stage of the interview you will engage in light conversation in order to break the ice. Topics can include the weather, your flight or drive in, or an activity or interest indicated on your resume. It is imperative that all during this time you come across as confident and mature. Be sure to give a firm handshake, look the interviewer in the eye, and follow his or her lead. This is the time to build rapport because decisions about suitability for the job are made in the first ten seconds to four minutes. The interviewer either likes or doesn't like you. You are judged by what you are wearing, your hair, makeup, jewelry, cologne or after shave, communication style, anxiety level, and overall personality.

If you are meeting with an interviewer for a position that you are well suited for, have taken the time to prepare for, and obviously want, chances are you will feel good about yourself as you enter the interview room, and if you do, you will make a positive impression.

Discussion   As the interview progresses, the interviewer will check out your work history in an attempt to learn more about your work and educational experiences. Typical early questions include "Tell me about yourself" and "Why did you choose your degree program?"

Future-oriented questions will be asked at some point in time. "What are your goals?" is a very common question. Your goals had better be related to the organization in some way. Employers want to be sure that your goals are in line with theirs.

Situational questions may be asked to assess how you would handle yourself in specific situations. Pay attention; they may offer a clue as to company concerns. Your job is to answer in such a way that the interviewer is put at ease. An example of a situational question is, "Mary, how would you react if one of your co-workers did not contribute his or her fair share?"

Most employers, depending on their level of interest in you, will try to sell you on the company, its products, and the reasons you should work for them—should they make an offer. Be attentive, show enthusiasm, and be ready to ask questions.

As the interview comes to a close, an employer will ask, "Do you have any questions for us?" Unless you want the interview process to end, ask some questions that are intelligent and well thought out. Employers want and expect you to do this. Asking questions shows your ability to analyze, your level of interest, and how much research you have done. Don't ask, "What is your benefit package like?" It is much too early in the process for that.

Some questions you may ask during the interview

1. Could you please describe a typical day on the job?

2. What kind of training does this organization offer?

3. Will I have a chance to meet my co-workers?

4. Are there specific skills or experiences that are beneficial in helping someone do well in this job?

5. Do most managers have advanced degrees? If so, which ones?

6. When will my first job performance evaluation take place?

7. Whom will I report to?

8. Does the company anticipate changing the current structure?

9. How much travel is normally expected?

10. How frequently do you relocate professional employees?

11. About how many individuals go through your training program each year?

12. Is it possible to transfer from one division to another?

13. How much input does a new employee have in the decision making relative to geographical placement in the first year?

14. What is the average age of top management?

15. What is the average time to get to _____ level in the career path?

16. What is the organization's policy on hiring from within?

17. Do employees usually work many hours of overtime?

18. Can I progress at my own pace or is it structured?

19. What is the average age of your first-level supervisors?

20. Is the sales growth in the new product line sustainable?

21. How much contact and exposure to management is there?

22. Tell me about your training programs.

23. When do the training programs begin?

24. What is the housing market for single people like?

25. Have there been any new product lines introduced recently?

26. Is a car provided for traveling?

27. How much independence is allowed for dress and appearance?

28. Is public transportation adequate?

29. What are the opportunities for personal growth?

30. What is the retention rate for people in this position?

31. Describe a typical first-year assignment.

32. What are the challenging aspects of the position?

33. What are the company's plans for future growth?

34. Is the company financially stable and sound?

35. What is the company's record of employment stability?

36. What are the industry trends? How have they affected this company?

37. How has this company fared during the recent recession?

38. What makes this organization different from its competitors?

39. What are the company's strengths and weaknesses?

40. How would you describe the company's culture and management style?

41. What are your expectations of new hires?

42. Describe the work environment.

43. Why do people want to work for your organization?

After the Interview   After the interview, sit down and collect your thoughts, reflect on how well you did, and ask yourself if there is anything else that you wished you had done or said. If there is something, you can include it in your thank-you letter. At the close of the interview, ask for the interviewer's business card. This will give you the name, address, and phone number of the company and the company representative. This is all you need to write a thank-you.

A thank-you note or letter is a courtesy, a marketing device to sell yourself one more time to an employer. It should be mailed out the day after you interview. If you are concerned about the mail delaying your letter, you may fax it. A thank-you note need not be long. It should express interest in the position, show appreciation for the opportunity to interview, and mention points you forgot to make during the interview. This letter should be more personal than the cover letter since you now know the person to whom you are writing. If you met with more than one person, be sure to thank each one individually.

Your note or letter can be typed on the same paper you used for your resume. You may use a handwritten card or formal note paper.

Important Interview Points   Body language or nonverbal behavior is an important element of the employment interview. Messages, whether intentional or not, are transmitted through the body. Some of these messages can be positive; others, negative. Many of the more apparent nonverbal messages are conveyed through eye contact, facial expressions, posture, and head, hand, and foot activity. Let's consider each of these. Then you rate your own "body language" and decide whether it is working for or against you.

Eye contact can range from a dead stare into the employer's eyes to total aversion of eye contact. Good eye contact is defined as looking at a person when he or she is speaking to you and while answering his or her questions. Good eye contact gives a message of attention and of being committed to communication. Looking everywhere but at the employer, constant blinking, or nervous twitches are to be avoided at all costs.

Facial expressions can range from a big grin or smile to a "stone face," with many possibilities in between. It is important to set the tone of the interview with a nice smile that conveys your pleasure and happiness to be there. An all-too-serious expression or nervous contortions convey an anxious message to the employer. Avoid these.

Posture. Sit up straight but be relaxed. You may want to sit at a slight angle. Avoid slouching or leaning back, as both convey a message of boredom and lack of interest.

Head, hand, and foot activity. Use your head to nod and follow the employer, your hands for handshaking and writing, if necessary, and your feet for walking into and out of the interview; otherwise, keep your activity level to a minimum. When people are nervous in an interview situation, they will tap their feet, play with rubber bands or pens, and rotate their head from side to side to relax the tension. Do not tap, play, or rotate if you want the job!

Finally, keep these points in mind:

• Let the interviewer begin and end the interview. Pay attention to clues and don't extend the time.

• Present a positive image; don't bash previous employers or focus on negative experiences.

• Dress appropriately for the industry in which you are applying.

• Be yourself.

If your three-pronged tactical approach to self-promotion is a good one, then you will be well on the way to success. It is your networking efforts, your resume, and your skill at interviewing that will differentiate you from the competition.

DISTRIBUTION

Section V

Dave Cassin,
Human Resource Manager,
Keane Inc.

Keane, Inc., utilizes a wide variety of sourcing avenues for recruiting entry-level candidates: employee referrals, job fairs, on-campus interviews, college professor referrals, college placement centers, campus/alumni newsletters, and newspaper ads. My approach to recruiting entry-level candidates is to utilize these sourcing avenues to develop and maintain a consistent network of contacts with various college representatives and students. I would like to list briefly some of the advantages these sourcing avenues offer from an employer's prospective.

Referrals by our own staff are an excellent source of candidates for two reasons. As an employer, we have the chance to gain additional insight into the candidate's compatibility with the organization, and the candidate has a great source of information about our firm and the position.

College job fairs are a very visible way to promote the company to a large number of candidates from many schools at one location in a timely manner. Job fairs allow both parties to exchange information briefly and to set up more comprehensive follow-up interviews.

On-campus interviews allow an employer to interview a number of prescreened candidates at an easily accessible location for the candidates.

College professors and placement center representatives can be excellent sources of candidates when they are informed about the desired qualifications for employment with our firm. They are also terrific information resources for the students.

Notices in college newspapers and alumni publications are a great way to increase our visibility to our targeted audience and generate inquiries about opportunities with Keane.

Newspaper advertisements are seen by a much larger audience and can attract students from other regions of the country who wish to return or relocate to the local area.

I feel that all these avenues should be utilized to attract qualified candidates. Candidates who take full advantage of these options and any other resources available to them early in their college years will be better prepared to make informed decisions about their professional careers.

Finding the Right Distribution Channels

The Place Factor

Now that you know how to develop both product and self-promotion strategies, it is time to move on to the third major component of the marketing mix—*distribution*, or *place* as it is referred to in some marketing texts. If you think of the word *place* instead of the word *distribution* you will easily understand its meaning as it applies to the human product. You must be in the right place at the right time if you are to get the attention of the right employers. Without the opportunity to "strut your stuff" there can be no job offer. Employers will not come knocking on your dorm or apartment door to find you; that is why this portion of your overall strategic self-marketing plan requires study of channels and selection of those that will get you where you want to be. Only through distribution can you display your professional image and use your impressive promotion skills.

There are many channels through which you can distribute resumes. All of these are available during the job search. It is up to you, however, to select the particular roads that are best suited to your situation. In order to do this, you must be aware of the various options.

A recent U.S. Bureau of Labor Management Board study of 495 major organizations employing almost four million people cited the following:

- Managers, professionals, and technical employees were generally hired through search firms or, for entry-level jobs, through college and university placement offices.

- Manufacturing and production employees were recruited from government agencies and employee referrals.

There are a number of distribution sources available while job searching. Analyze all of them. Do not rely solely on want ads or any other single source. Since want ads are not the resource of choice for most employers who seek college graduates, do not use them as a primary distribution tool.

A recent survey, done by the Erdlen and Bogard Group of Wellesley, Massachusetts, indicated that many professional and managerial employees who were laid off at mid-career found new positions through the following:

- Networking   34.1 percent
- Advertisements   23.4 percent
- Employment agencies   17.1 percent
- Direct contacts   6.2 percent
- Executive search firms   4.6 percent
- Job Fairs   2.7 percent
- Miscellaneous   11.9 percent

The American Management Association also did a survey. Its findings show that the recruiting sources that generate the most number of candidates for their members include:

- Newspaper advertising   39 percent
- Employee referrals   15 percent
- In-house search   10 percent
- Campus recruiting   9 percent
- Contingency agencies   8 percent
- Job fairs   7 percent
- Trade publications   5 percent
- Search firms   3 percent
- Other   4 percent

The following examples illustrate the different recruiting methods used by different companies.

Company X hires two hundred trainees every year. The purpose is always to have available fifty good managers for existing positions throughout the organization. Each year, if the economy is stable, the company's human resource staff interviews fifteen hundred college seniors on eighty campuses, invites five hundred of them for in-house interviews with department managers, and makes offers to three hundred finalists. All this is done in order to reach the company hiring goal of two hundred trainees a year. Company X holds information sessions at selected campuses throughout the country, advertises in the various career centers, and posts announcements of upcoming visits at each institution where it plans to recruit.

Company Y, a leader in the insurance industry, is growing rapidly and plans to open fifteen new offices nationwide in the coming year. In order to hire sixty new sales managers, the company plans to use advertisements in local papers and referrals.

Company Z, a small marketing research firm, needs someone to do research and write proposals. The CEO expects to rely on a search firm to locate and screen candidates since she has little time to do this herself. She will also call her contact at an area college in the hope of finding a new graduate or even a co-op student who might be able to do the work. Then, remembering a young man with the right qualifications who contacted her a few months ago, she decides also to call him.

Companies X, Y, and Z are all offering positions for which you may qualify. How do you find out about them? How do you position yourself for that all-important interview and land a job? Understanding the various distribution channels will help you develop proper strategies and will start you on the road to employment.

Major Distribution Channels

The major distribution channels are:

- Want ads
- Job fairs
- College and university faculty
- Employment agencies
- Professional associations
- Government agencies
- On-campus recruitment
- Telephone books/business directories/chamber of commerce guides
- Networking
- Co-operative education/internship programs

Want ads

Located in the "Help Wanted" section of newspapers, want ads are a bountiful source of potential jobs. Employers place want ads for the purpose of attracting candidates to fill openings. Want ads list all of the criteria you will need to meet in order to be considered for an interview. Information in the ad usually includes the job title, education and skill requirements, experience needed, and pertinent employer information, such as address, contact name, and a brief description of the company's product or service. Telephone numbers may or may not be listed. Even if listed, the ad may include a statement such as "no phone calls, please." It is always best to follow instructions. When a phone number is given without any instructions, it is a good idea to end your cover letter with a final sentence indicating that you will follow up your response with a phone call in a week or ten days.

Coupled with the use of other distribution channels, want ads can be beneficial. They are good sources of current job opportunities. A positive feature of want ads is that they only appear if the jobs are available and current. Through researching want-ad sections of newspapers, you will also be able to identify trends in the employment market, salary ranges, and various job requirements. This channel, therefore, can serve a dual purpose in your job search. Extend your want-ad search beyond your local paper. Read the nearest big-city papers at least once a week, preferably the Sunday edition, and visit your local library. With the help of a librarian, identify periodicals, trade papers, and publications in your field. These usually have want-ad sections that are targeted at people who hold college degrees.

There are some negative features of newspaper want ads:

- They only represent 10 to 20 percent of available openings at any given time.

- They generate hundreds of responses, creating a very competitive situation.

- Success is only possible if the applicant's background matches the employer's exact requirements.

- Response is slow, often leading to frustration.

- Those who rely solely on want ads are usually not as successful at finding a position as quickly as those who use other sources in combination with want ads.

Job fairs   Job fairs may be sponsored by the government, private business, nonprofit organizations, educational institutions, chambers of commerce, or professional groups. The primary purpose of these fairs is to bring employers and job searchers together and create a match. Some job fairs are discipline specific, geared to those with technical backgrounds or to social service, health care, or financial service professionals; others are geographically oriented. Regardless of the name used, Career Exposition, Career Day, or Career Fair, a job fair is a job fair, and the purpose is the same.

Prior to attending a job fair, be sure that you know why you are attending. Is your purpose to gain information for later use in the job search or are you planning to speak with employers about current openings? Whatever the reason, it is imperative that you be prepared. Remain professional at all times and communicate your intentions to each company representative with whom you speak.

Employers are not always looking to fill current openings. Some may be looking to develop a pool of candidates for the future. Whether it is your desire to land a position now, in six months, or a year from now, the rapport that you develop with the company recruiter will lay down the groundwork for future communications. If he or she is impressed with you, chances are that communications will continue. If you do not impress the recruiter, chances for future contact with that particular person are unlikely. As previously mentioned, an impression is established in four minutes or less and almost all decisions concerning your future prospects with employers are made based on that first impression. At job fairs as well as in all channels, never forget the importance of the initial meeting.

There are some positive aspects of job fairs, such as:

- easy accessibility

- the opportunity to sell yourself in person

- the chance to see many employers who are actively recruiting in one place

There are also negative aspects. These include:

- competition from many candidates with qualifications equal to or better than yours

- the possibility of misrepresenting yourself because your attitude is less serious than it would be during a private interview

College and university faculty

Throughout your college experiences, you have had the opportunity to interact with at least twenty to forty faculty members. With some, you developed a comfortable relationship. If you have also proven your academic ability to those you became close to, they may be willing to go "the extra mile" and make a referral to one of their contacts, either in the college community or elsewhere. Be sure to approach faculty with whom you have a positive rapport and let them know of your future plans and aspirations.

Many college seniors include the "faculty road" in their distribution strategy. It should also be given consideration by job seekers or career changers who have been out of school for a number of years. "Old professors" enjoy hearing from former students with whom they had a special relationship. Since most members of the academic community have contacts in their field, they often hear of potential openings before they even occur. Consider this source whether your degree is current, five or ten years old, or even older.

Employment agencies

There are a variety of employment agencies available to you as job searchers. These can be broken down into four main groups. It is important that you learn the major differences between them. The list includes (1) headhunters/executive recruiters, (2) temporary agencies, (3) permanent placement agencies, and (4) career planning or career counseling offices. Understanding the basic differences between each will save both you and the agency representative time and frustration. You should also know who will be paying the agency, the employer or you, before you decide which ones to include in your distribution plan.

Executive recruiters or headhunters are primarily interested in working for and with established professionals who have experience and expertise to offer an employer. They generally seek out employed professionals in hopes of convincing them to leave their present positions and take jobs with the agency's client companies.

If they are successful, the agency and the agency recruiter will receive a preestablished commission. Since most executive recruiters/headhunters are paid by their employer clients who are looking to fill upper-level positions, they are rarely interested in the traditional new college graduate, who has limited experience. The advice for new graduates, therefore, is to give little, if any, consideration to this distribution path. It is a good strategy tool, however, for career changers.

Temporary agencies place individuals in temporary full-time or part-time positions that can range from one day to one year. The only time a temporary agency may be of some service to you in marketing your college degree is if you are looking to gain experience, develop particular skills, or find a special way to penetrate a special organization. Employers usually pay the fees for this service. During the recession of the early 1990s, temporary placement agencies played a major role for some college graduates who had problems finding first career jobs because of the downsizing in so many industries.

Permanent placement agencies have grown in recent years as employers search for special individuals to fill specific positions. Generally, employers pay the agency a fee, usually a percentage of the first year salary paid to the person who is hired. If you decide to use a permanent placement agency, find out who pays the fee—you, the employer, or both—before you make a commitment. Then, base your decision on this information.

Many individuals who sign up with a private agency become frustrated after a short period of time because they never receive information about job openings. Unless you offer a "hot" skill or meet the requirements for a current order the agency is looking to fill, it is likely that your file will sit in a drawer. If you are not paying the fee, then the agency representative will generally not go out and look for positions that meet your background. If you decide to use a private permanent placement agency, be sure to discuss their assistance plans and establish a time frame for periodic follow-up meetings before signing a contract. If you don't get the right information up front, just forget this method of distribution.

Career planning and placement/career counseling agencies will actually create your strategic marketing plan for you. They "do it all" for a fee. Their services include career counseling, resume writing, and typing assistance. They also provide you with company listings and teach you the basics of the job search. There are some very reputable career counselors in every community. If you feel that a professional can create a better strategic marketing plan for you than you can for yourself, and you have between $1,000 and $2,000 to spend on marketing yourself, then consider this type of agency, *but* only after you have done a thorough check of the agency's credentials and placement history. Also, before making the decision to invest in this resource, ask yourself the question "Can a stranger do a better job of analyzing and marketing me than I can?" Consider your answer carefully.

Professional associations   Almost every industry or career field has a professional association. Once you identify your field of choice, you can contact the association to find out if it publishes a newsletter, how often it holds meetings, and where meetings are held. If you are a student, you need to find out if you have access to its publications and meetings. A newsletter will provide you with information about your chosen field and may even include notices of current job opportunities. At meetings and conferences, you can make contacts who may be very helpful in launching your career. Association newsletters and conferences are wonderful sources for gathering job information that may not be available in traditional channels like want ads or job fairs. Resources such as the *Encyclopedia of Associations* can be helpful in identifying associations that are related to your particular career field.

Alumni

College and university alumni offices offer assistance through alumni associations, publications, or both. They can also give you lists of alumni by geographic location and, sometimes, by profession, so you can get in touch with them personally. The importance of utilizing alumni in the job search can not be overstated. Alumni will provide you with information and contact names other than their own in their given field or community, if for no other reason then the good feeling they get from helping someone from their alma mater.

Cold calling or direct contact

Cold calling is at the opposite end of the spectrum from using the want-ad channel. Cold calling can be done in person, over the phone, through the mail—or any combination thereof. In cold calling, you approach individuals with whom you have had no previous contact and apply for positions without knowing if an actual opening exists. The direct contact method—sending a letter and resume or calling a company without knowing if there are openings—is a popular approach for many college graduates. It can be somewhat successful if you identify a contact person and develop some rapport with him or her prior to sending your cover letter and resume.

A recent survey by the Employment Management Association reveals that members rarely create positions for applicants who write in cold (only 2 percent). The survey also showed that cold resumes and cover letters sent to the line managers get a 97 percent greater response than those sent to the human resources department. If using this channel choice, your best tactic is probably to write to a line manager and hope that your first impression is really exceptional. Direct contact does allow you to assume the initiative and gives you an opportunity to demonstrate your creativity and resourcefulness.

Through cold calling, you may be able to uncover an opening that didn't exist or wasn't advertised, and you may be considered for the position you uncovered. If you make a great first impression, it is also possible that a job may even be created for you.

When using this self-distribution channel, determine the key department heads and write to them. Avoid the human resources department, as its role is to screen. Human resources can stop your search if there are no known openings in your area of interest.

Cold calling requires that you create the opportunity, assume the initiative, and as stated, be creative and resourceful. Identify companies of interest, identify the key contact person, research the company, and make the direct contact. There is no doubt that this process requires perseverance and the ability to handle rejection. Because of this, many people shy away from the direct contact channel, which is all the more reason it can be more successful for those who do use it.

Libraries are excellent resources when using direct contact. Directories for every industry from accounting to travel and tourism, and all others in between, with lists of names of members and contact persons, can be found on their shelves. In some cases, directories may be the only way to find out about companies in your field of interest.

Government agencies

Both federal and state governments offer assistance to job searchers. Services include career days, job publications and listings, testing, and career planning and placement assistance. The Office of Personnel Management is an agency of the federal government, and the Division of Employment Security is a division of the state government. Job searchers seeking work with the federal government should contact the nearest OPM to learn more about the current Career America Program and also the ins and outs of the application process for federal government employment. The DES posts positions for both government and private business.

On-campus recruitment

This is one channel that everyone who is about to receive a degree should consider, even though only nine out of one hundred students interviewed on campus end up on the interviewer's payroll. Of the one hundred interviewed, about twenty-seven get a second interview and sixteen, a job offer. Half the job offers are accepted.

Although there has been a decrease in on-campus recruiting in recent years, there are still many employers who make their annual pilgrimage to their campuses of choice. If this service is offered through your career center, take advantage of it. Interview with as many employers as possible, selecting those companies that interest you because they offer positions and career opportunities that interest you. Companies looking to fill positions with new graduates go directly to the college and university career centers where they know an excellent pool of potential candidates await them. Never again will it be this easy to gain access to such a variety of employers.

Be aware of the fact that employers are very careful in selecting the colleges where they recruit. They usually choose institutions that graduate the type of students who fit their specific needs, such as engineering students for engineering firms and marketing students for marketing firms. Companies with intensive training programs, however, are interested in all graduates regardless of their college major, as long as they can communicate well and have excellent interpersonal skills. Employers also tend to visit schools where they have hired graduates who have become successful employees.

Many colleges are involved in off-campus recruiting programs. These are alternatives to on-campus programs. Off-campus recruiting is done regionally by employers who can meet with students from many college and universities at one time and in one place, rather than on each campus in the area.

Directories and guides Telephone books, business directories, and chamber of commerce guides list employers alphabetically, by type of business, or both. Study these books; they can provide leads to companies of which you may be unaware. Information includes address and telephone numbers of all area businesses and nonprofit organizations. They also provide information on the number of competitors in the area. If using this channel, be sure you call each company you target for a contact name before beginning your communications.

Networking It has been said that 75 percent of all jobs are acquired through personal contacts (better known as networking). Thus, traditional employment sources such as use of college career offices, employment agencies, and want ads are taking a back seat to self-developed leads. The topic of networking was discussed earlier in great detail as a self-promotion strategy. It can also be considered a distribution strategy. Networking during the job search is more than merely a way of "getting the word out." It will also provide you with personal channels through which to distribute yourself to potential employers.

Co-operative education and internship programs

Co-operative education/internship programs are pregraduation distribution options at some colleges and universities. These channels allow students to sample careers while still undergraduates, by working in their chosen field either part or full time during a semester or summer. At some institutions students can alternate between the classroom and the workplace.

Often, these programs become the first step on the career ladder since many employers hire previous co-op/intern students at graduation time. Employers like to hire from this group because its members are familiar with both the company image and work patterns.

Self-distribution serves only one purpose. It is a positioning strategy aimed at heading you in the right direction so that you will be in the right place at the right time to start or continue the climb up your chosen career ladder. A good product needs good distribution.

RETURN ON INVESTMENT

Section VI

Maureen Molen,
Vice-President of Human Resources,
Doral Hotels and Resort Management Corporation

In preparing for the interviewing process, you should conduct a thorough analysis of a company's needs, taking into consideration both current and future goals. It is these needs and goals that help determine salary levels.

Because wages make up such an enormous segment of our budget, we cannot start interviewing potential employees until we know how much we can offer candidates.

When we find it necessary to fill a position from outside our organization, we review and update job descriptions and performance standards. We also establish competitive salary ranges for our positions. Throughout the interviewing process, we look for the best-qualified individual whose education and experiences meet the position specifications. We expect to attract rising stars who are enthusiastic and energetic, have strong team leadership abilities, are solid citizens, and have a natural service orientation.

Occasionally during a search, we find it necessary to adjust salary ranges as the marketplace and candidate pool fluctuate. We are committed to only hiring and retaining employees who fit the Doral profile. We offer a competitive compensation package and the opportunity to grow with a dynamic hotel management company.

Pricing

10

According to the U.S. Census Bureau, a college degree is worth 39 percent more in annual earnings than a high school diploma. Amortize that over your career life and it becomes pretty impressive. In addition to your degree, it is your college major that will help determine exactly how much you are worth. Engineers generally make much more than social workers; physicians, more than pharmacists; and lawyers, more than economists. In 1973 the difference in earning power for a college graduate was twice as great as for a high school graduate. In the 1990s the difference has grown to four times as much. It will continue to grow each year. Based on the most recent U.S. Census Bureau information, the answer to the question, "Is the price worth the potential rewards?" is a definite *yes*! Statistics show that a college degree is still a good investment.

As a candidate in the job-search process, you are well aware that your education has been a major investment of time, energy, and money for both you and your family. What kind of return will you make on this investment? The following discussion will help you decide what you are worth to yourself and to an employer. In determining your worth, look at your personal financial needs as *one determinant* of the value of your investment. To begin this task, ask yourself the following questions:

1. How much money will I need to meet my basic needs (food, housing, transportation) the first year in a new job?

2. What do I think my skills, experience, and degree are worth in the marketplace?

3. What dollar figure do I hope to get and what am I willing to accept?

It is common for many college graduates to have inflated expectations regarding salary. This is a source of potential inner conflict when the salary offered by the employer you hoped would hire you is not enough to cover your basic needs as you defined them and is not in keeping with the value you have placed on your degree. To gain a better understanding of a reasonable starting salary, you should utilize the readily available resources discussed in this section.

Once you have determined the salary you would like, the next step is to determine if it is realistic in terms of the current market. Researching salary statistics is not difficult. There are a number of resources you can study in order to gain a better understanding of the worth of your degree, experience, and skills. Through research you will be able to establish a low and high salary range for the type of position, the industry, and the geographic area of your choice. Your college major will also play an important role in determining your worth. When putting a price on yourself, consider, too, your GPA, your experience, and market supply and demand. Right or wrong, many employers are willing to pay you more if you hold a degree from a prestigious university. If you are a graduate of a little-known college and your qualifications for the position in question are the same as your competitors from an Ivy League school, you may have to fight harder for the starting salary you want by creating a better overall marketing mix than the competition. This is another reason why taking a marketing approach to career planning is so vital.

Even if your degree is from the "best of the best," it is the use of a strategic marketing plan that will help you gain the compensation package you are seeking. No degree, no matter what its source, will override an expert self-marketing mix created by job candidates who have done their homework and know all the tactics and tools. Researching salary statistics will give you a base to start your pricing strategy and help you determine your worth from an employer's perspective.

Salary Information Resources

When establishing their salary levels, employers research statistics such as those compiled by the College Placement Council (CPC), a national association of colleges and universities. The CPC survey incorporates offers made to graduates at 450 campuses nationwide. The survey is the largest of its kind and provides employers with a benchmark for making decisions on proper pay for college graduates in their first career jobs.

If a college or university belongs to both CPC and its regional arm, its career centers have access to the CPC salary survey. The regional arms are the Eastern College Placement Association (ECPO), the Middle Atlantic Placement Association (MAPA), the Midwest College Placement Association (MCPA), the Rocky Mountain College Placement Association (RMPCA), the Southern College Placement Association (SCPA), the SouthWest Placement Association (SWPA), and the Western College Placement Association (WCPA). As stated, the CPC survey compiles reports from 450 college and university career planning and placement offices nationwide. Reports are issued four times annually and provide the most up-to-date information available. The salary information is presented in a number of formats by major, industry, or function. It is also broken down by sex and years of experience.

Many employers are comfortable paying an average of the starting salaries on the list. Others recognize that they will earn a better return on their investment over a longer period of time by paying above-average salaries. Above-average salaries tend to create a feeling of employee loyalty from the first day on the job.

Many college career centers conduct an annual salary survey that reports earnings of their own graduates from the previous year. Some career centers also do five-year surveys in conjunction with alumni organizations. If an annual survey is conducted by your school, its results will give you a fair idea of starting salaries for graduates from your institution. Most salary surveys, whether done by a college career office or an organization like CPC, are excellent resources for developing the pricing portion of your marketing mix. Career counselors can also put you in touch with alumni, employers, professional or trade associations, and personnel agencies.

Alumni who are working in positions or industries of interest to you can provide you with realistic salary ranges offered by their particular employers. Remember, just because Joe was offered $28,000 by his employer when he graduated, your offer may be different. Not only is it a different year, but your geographic choice may not be the same as his.

Professional and trade association members are always aware of current salaries in their fields. These people are excellent resources for determining salary ranges. Resources like the National Trade and Professional Associations of the United States will help you to target the associations in your area of interest so you can get names of contact persons. Then you can either write or call them to get the salary information that will help you in your self-marketing plan.

Employment agency professionals are also knowledgeable about current salary ranges. Some may be willing to share their knowledge with you, especially if they know that you are looking to test reality against expectations.

Negotiating

When, during the interview, the issue of salary range is brought up by the interviewer, the question usually asked is, "What salary are you looking for?" There are a number of ways that you can respond:

1. "What salary range has been established for this particular position?"

2. "What are the parameters for negotiation?"

3. "Am I correct in assuming that _____ is the industry figure for starting salaries in this job?"

4. "It's the total package that interests me. What exactly does your benefit package include?"

5. "I'm more interested in a position where I can prove myself and develop skills than I am in salary."

6. "I cannot accept less than $_____. With this amount I can survive while giving my all to the company."

When employers ask about your salary needs, they are trying to determine whether you fall into their established ranges. If you have done your homework, you should be able to provide an answer that is acceptable. Your ability to do this will show your understanding of the realities of the working world, the times, the location, and the industry.

Remember, that to a certain extent, salaries are negotiable. If a company is really interested in you and your abilities, its representative will come up with the money necessary to hire you. If possible, wait for the employer to bring up the issue of salary negotiation. It has been said that whoever brings up salary first "loses." Losing should not be in your game plan. It is also important that you stay within an appropriate range based on the research that you have done during your preparation phase, but don't undersell yourself. Aim high; you can always settle for less. In aiming high, however, be sure you do not put yourself out of the game with your first "ask"!

In a situation where a low salary is a major concern for you and will have an impact on your final decision to take a position, it is best to bring the issue up and talk about it up front. In this case don't be afraid of "losing" since you cannot take the position anyway unless your needs are met. If the employer can't meet your needs, there is no sense in pursuing the job further.

Fringe Benefits

Fringe benefits are an important part of the actual compensation for any job. The program offered by individual employers should be studied when evaluating a job. For every $100 employees receive in direct salary or wages, it costs employers an estimated additional $40 to cover fringe benefits such as pensions, health insurance, vacations, and other retirement options. This is an impressive figure and job seekers should keep "hidden payroll" benefits in mind when considering a job offer.

Statutory benefits are required by law for all employers. They include (1) social security (for retirement later), (2) worker's compensation (in case of an injury on the job), and (3) unemployment insurance (to be used in case of a layoff). The only cost to you in this category is a portion of social security. This is 7.65 percent of your salary. The amount is matched by your employer.

Vacations/holidays. Paid holidays average ten days a year with most employers—but some offer as many as twenty. A few employers even offer a week's vacation between Christmas and New Year's Day. Almost all employers provide paid vacations, generally starting with two weeks for the first few years and building up to four or five weeks after fifteen to twenty years of employment. Currently, about a third of all employers offer unpaid maternity leave. A few offer paid leave during this period. Because of pressure from women's organizations, others will include some type of maternity leave in their fringe-benefit package in the future.

Pension plans. Retirement programs that supplement social security coverage are offered by larger employers as well as by some smaller companies. Money paid by your employers into your pension plan is generally not part of your taxable earnings.

Health insurance. Employer-sponsored health insurance is offered to 90 percent of all full-time employees. In view of the increasing cost of these programs (often as high as $4,000 for family coverage), more employees are being asked to share the cost of the premiums. Some plans pay all the expenses; others, for lower premiums, are only concerned with the unusual or catastrophic bills. This is one benefit that potential employees should always look for. Without adequate health insurance, a person or a family could face financial disaster from just one significant illness or accident.

Dental insurance. Many organizations offer dental insurance. The value of this benefit cannot be overstated. Employers will generally cover most of the cost of the insurance.

Life insurance. Most large organizations provide some form of life insurance coverage, generally paid in-full by the employer. Usually the amount of this benefit will depend upon the employee's salary and job level. Often it is equal to one or two years' salary, paid to the employee's beneficiary upon the death of the employee.

Other benefits. Many large firms help with tuition and other expenses incurred by employees taking college courses. This is especially true if the courses relate to the employee's job. A few companies offer scholarship help to children of employees. Some organizations help with child care expenses, and about one-sixth of all major employers offer some form of profit sharing, which enables employees to benefit financially if the firm has a good year.

Cafeteria plans are flexible benefit plans that allow employees to make some choices among the options offered. For some, child care is not important, but current vacation time is. Many don't need health insurance because the family is already covered by a spouse. Choices and options are not unlimited, but some selection by each employee is possible.

It is important when setting a price on any product or service to take into consideration the preparation costs of the product, the ratio between supply and demand, and the effect of uncontrollable variables, such as a recession or an unexpected political upheaval, on the pricing structure. These considerations are just as important when setting a price on yourself. You are affected by your preparation costs (education), supply and demand (the number of openings versus the number of viable candidates for each opening), and any number of uncontrollable social, economic, or political variables, which can open or close doors at a moments notice.

In determining your worth, never forget that employers and job searchers have different sets of criteria from each other when establishing salary ranges. Try and put yourself in the employers' shoes when deciding your real value in the marketplace.

POST-CAMPAIGN BEHAVIOR

Mary Jean Basileo,
Employment Manager
Saks Fifth Avenue

You control the destiny of your career. Once you have successfully achieved the job you have sought you must continually enhance your basic skill level while always striving for new and challenging experiences.

Every day you should approach your job with the perspective of not only meeting the day's objectives, but also asking how you can make a significant contribution. You must be willing to approach each daily activity, no matter how big or small, with the attitude that you will take your job to a higher level of commitment and expertise. This is what will set you apart. This is the approach that will get you ahead.

Always remain aware of your company's philosophy and objectives. Regardless of what area of the company you work in, maintain a constant awareness of where your company is in the industry, who the competition is and a knowledge of general economic events that impact your organization's business and goals. Flexibility, adaptability and a positive attitude will also be key components in the individual who successfully moves up the career ladder.

Throughout your career, always keep an open mind and welcome opportunities within your organization that will broaden your knowledge and expertise. Every new experience can only enhance your marketability within and outside your organization and industry. Your mobility will be determined by the skills and knowledge you acquire.

Many occupations share diverse characteristics and many companies welcome individuals with varied and nontraditional skills to their industry. Be confident in your accomplishments and what you can bring to another job.

A job is what you make of it. If you take it for face value, that is all it ever will be. Therefore, your career strategy does not end once you get a job; it is an ongoing process at which you must always work.

After You've Landed That Job 11

You were introduced earlier to the product life cycle, which starts with the introductory stage, moves to the growth stage, then to maturity, and finally to decline. In order to succeed, you need to be aware of expectations at each stage, both yours and your employers. Above all else, you must give careful consideration to your performance during the introductory stage. How you act, learn, and progress the first year on the job will determine your movement from the first stage to the second stage and beyond.

Stage I is characterized by high energy and a willingness to learn and contribute. Employers expect a lot for a little. New employees who play by the rules tend to move up their career ladders quicker than those who don't. Laziness, ineptness, poor use of skills, inability to learn, or personality problems during the first year on the job will surely lead to job loss or stagnation. Either should be an unacceptable option to an ambitious individual.

What Employers Expect

A *positive attitude* means more than anything else when beginning your career. You should start a new position with the attitude that both you and your employer will gain something from your employment. This is a new era. The days are gone when employers expect or even want you to work in their organization until the age of retirement, so don't worry about "twenty-five years from now." What you do your first year on the job will serve you well in any company or in your own business. Worry about the here and now! It's clear that many employers are not as loyal to their older employees as they once were. With the increase in layoffs, cutbacks, and voluntary early retirement programs, 25 percent of currently unemployed people are fifty years old or older. If you prepare yourself properly during the introductory stage of your career and do your assigned work because you want to and because you also believe it will help you create your own career path, the next thirty-five years will be years of movement and maturity, regardless of the "uncontrollables."

Give your first position all that you've got. Develop your skills, learn the ins and outs of the business, and, whether you plan to stay with the company or not, you will move to stage II. Studies show that the average length of stay for new graduates in their first job is only eighteen months to two years. Use position number one as a stepping stone to your future.

Loyalty. Employers expect loyalty. Support your manager and don't misuse the company's time or money. Above all, don't be negative through words or actions. Show a willingness to do whatever it takes to get the job done. Work for the good of the company. You should be at the customer's beck and call, if necessary; photocopy if asked to, and always deal with difficult people, including managers, peers, and customers, as diplomatically as possible. Learn to recognize situations when it is beneficial to nod your head, say yes, and move on, even if you have to bite your tongue. Your day will come!

As a new employee, be competitive and show that you are good if not better than your peers. A competitive spirit can act as an excellent motivator and is good for all concerned. While showing competitive spirit, also remain a member of the team. No one likes a show-off. Part of a positive attitude is to take the initiative to get the job done. Don't wait to be told what to do, and don't be afraid to ask how to do it in the best possible way.

Recognize that you will always be subject to criticism

and corrections as you move through your career life cycle. Be prepared to handle both in a positive manner. More often than not you will gain from advice, and diplomatic communication will help you maintain or further develop positive relationships.

Good interpersonal and communication skills. From the day you are employed, you will meet many new people. The impression you make can follow you throughout your career; therefore, make sure that your stage I impression is a positive one. Learn all you can about the other employees in the company, their position, and power status within the organization. Avoid saying something that you will regret later down the road.

On the job you will encounter people from various educational and socioeconomic backgrounds. They may be clients, colleagues, or managers. Respect and recognize their differences in all communication because this will aid you in developing good rapport. Work on your interpersonal communication skills; they may become somewhat different from those that served you well during your college years.

Employers are impressed with new employees who write and speak well. If you have excellent writing and verbal skills, you will gain recognition from clients, fellow workers, and superiors.

Another important interpersonal skill that can surface during the introductory stage of your career is your ability, if in disagreement, to negotiate your point. You should always search for a win-win situation, so, in discussions, always be sensitive to others. Trying to be right all of the time may hurt your chances for success in either the short or the long run.

Understanding your own experience level. Unfortunately, many of today's college graduates have a tendency to want to start at the top. They also believe that they are entitled to this expectation. Starting at the top is most unlikely unless entering a family business, and even then it is not typical.

Some older graduates with a great deal of experience may be able to start in the growth or even maturity stage of their career life cycle, especially if they were employed for many years by the same employer who was only waiting for them to earn a college degree before promoting them to a high- or higher-level professional position.

Each inexperienced newcomer has to pay his or her dues—it's part of the plan. The first job out of college is a golden opportunity for developing skills, learning as much as possible about the field, being trained, and learning from mistakes. Of course, employers will measure newcomers and their output against other employees. Be prepared to bite the bullet and do some "gruntwork." It will pay off.

The ability to go with transition. The transition from college to the workplace is not always smooth, and it is never easy. Initially, you may be treated as if you have little knowledge or ability. This can lead to frustration and discontent. Be patient. It is imperative that you look at the big picture, recognizing your present place in the company. During the introduction phase, determine what is expected of you, ask questions, and make productive use of your time. As the weeks and months pass, the company's expectations will fall in line with your own, and within three to six months, you will be expected to get the job done with little or no assistance. By the time this happens, you will also be able to do it.

Understand your career goals and how your first job will help you climb to the next stage—growth. Make your first position work for you. Develop good work habits, get used to getting up on time, getting to work on time, and staying alert and productive for the entire working day, whether it is eight hours or longer. Mastering this part of the transition is imperative for success in your career.

While maintaining a focus on your career goals, don't fail to lose sight of your employer's goals or your role in helping the company to achieve its desired level of success. An element of industriousness, a touch of anxiety, and a knack for problem solving will take you far.

Decision-making ability. Of all the skills it is essential to master in the introduction stage, decision making is the most critical if you want to move into the growth stage. Managers must make decisions. If you do not show that you can do this you will not succeed beyond your first job. By studying all of the available information and considering the players, you will be able to do your best. Everyone has to make decisions at one time or another, and mistakes should be few and far between if you do your homework. Show that you are capable of performing this extremely critical management task by taking risks early in your career. One mistake is never fatal. Sometime in the past, your manager had to make his or her first decision and will not understand continued reluctance on your part. Decision making goes with the territory. Accept it or stay in a dead-end first job forever.

Office Politics

You can ignore office politics, but you cannot escape from them. Everywhere you work you will encounter political intrigue. It is part of human nature. Since it is best to avoid involvement until you know who is who, you can spend time observing some political types. These are the players who always seem to know the right thing to say at the right time. You can learn a great deal from them.

Observe, but don't get involved at this stage of your career. Above all else, avoid those who practice illegitimate politics; they will get you nowhere. Don't ever compromise your integrity, and always remember that playing politics is not a substitute for a job well done. Don't spend more time getting involved in the informal organization than in the formal one because politics can take a great deal of time and energy away from your job. Your ability to handle both your work and office politics, while becoming a team player, is the key to success during the introductory stage, as well as throughout your career life cycle.

What Employees Expect

Mentors. New employees always hope to find mentors who are knowledgeable. Seek out someone you respect and trust and whom you can ask for advice. A good mentor can also act as a sounding board for your ideas. Mentors have knowledge of both the formal and informal structure of the workplace, know the players, and can assist with your development. Since career development starts during stage I of your career life cycle, look for a mentor who will help you grow professionally.

Networking was discussed in great detail earlier. Not mentioned at that time was the importance of networking throughout your life. Never stop making contacts who can help you move along your career path. Peers, supervisors, clients, competitors, former professors, or anyone who knows and respects you becomes part of the lifelong network that is your own personal public relations agency.

Performance evaluation. Some employers provide a performance evaluation after an employee has been on the job for six months. Others wait until the end of the first year. Since it is important for both parties to go through the evaluation process, ask for an evaluation if it is not on the agenda. Everyone deserves a pat on the back for a job well done. It is also essential to know what you may be doing that needs improvement. Evaluation goes beyond reviewing the past period's performance. It is also a time to determine new duties, objectives, and career goals. Evaluations set standards, provide motivation and direction, and act as a measure against which the next period's performance can be judged. If you are to move up the career ladder, you must know where you stand at each step. You have a right to expect a periodic evaluation from every employer throughout your career life cycle.

The corporate culture is the sum total of every aspect of the corporate environment: the way people dress, the way they act (on and off the job), the management style that is encouraged, and the number of work hours that are expected. You may find after six months or a year in your first job that the corporate culture and your personal culture do not match. If that is the case, then it is time to look for a new work environment. Some people search for years before finding the right match. Changing jobs during your early career years is an acceptable tactic, provided each move brings you closer to personal satisfaction and is not an escape from responsibility or advancement opportunities. When your culture and the corporate culture do match, your movement toward achievement of your goals is assured.

Moving On

As you move through your career life cycle you may have to repackage transferable skills or completely change career direction. Changes in the economy, demographics, or world geography, as well as technological advances, affect employment needs and the profiles of American workers. When America moved from an agrarian to an industrial economy, farmers became factory workers. As we moved from an industrial to a technology-based economy, factory workers learned how to operate computers. With today's emphasis on a service economy, interpersonal and communication skills are in greater demand by employers in every field than ever before.

Movement means change and change means movement. There are no more cigar store Indians perched outside of general stores, for there are no more general stores. Don't let yourself become an item of the past. Repackage, re-learn, recycle, and your career movement will reflect the new opportunities brought about by the one thing that is certain in all societies—CHANGE!!

The growth industries of the twenty-first century may not even be in existence today. You may face many detours in the years ahead before you finally reach maturity, the third career stage where you can attain self-esteem. Don't be afraid to transfer your skills or your image. The repackaging information in section 2 will help you do this so that your career life cycle will peak at stage III and never reach the decline stage. Decline is only an option for those who do not practice the principles of self-marketing throughout their lives. All others will succeed.